Investigating Wireless Networks and Devices

EC-Council | Press

Volume 5 of 5 mapping to

C | HFI™

Computer | Hacking Forensic INVESTIGATOR

Certification

COURSE TECHNOLOGY
CENGAGE Learning™

Australia • Brazil • Japan • Korea • Mexico • Singapore • Spain • United Kingdom • United States

COURSE TECHNOLOGY
CENGAGE Learning™

Investigating Wireless Networks and Devices: EC-Council | Press

Course Technology/Cengage Learning Staff:

Vice President, Career and Professional Editorial: Dave Garza

Director of Learning Solutions: Matthew Kane

Executive Editor: Stephen Helba

Managing Editor: Marah Bellegarde

Editorial Assistant: Meghan Orvis

Vice President, Career and Professional Marketing: Jennifer Ann Baker

Marketing Director: Deborah Yarnell

Marketing Manager: Erin Coffin

Marketing Coordinator: Shanna Gibbs

Production Director: Carolyn Miller

Production Manager: Andrew Crouth

Content Project Manager: Brooke Greenhouse

Senior Art Director: Jack Pendleton

EC-Council:

President | EC-Council: Sanjay Bavisi

Sr. Director US | EC-Council: Steven Graham

For product information and technology assistance, contact us at
Cengage Learning Customer & Sales Support, 1-800-354-9706

For permission to use material from this text or product,
submit all requests online at **www.cengage.com/permissions**.
Further permissions questions can be e-mailed to
permissionrequest@cengage.com

Library of Congress Control Number: 2009933551

ISBN-13: 978-1-4354-8353-8

ISBN-10: 1-4354-8353-7

Cengage Learning
5 Maxwell Drive
Clifton Park, NY 12065-2919
USA

Cengage Learning is a leading provider of customized learning solutions with office locations around the globe, including Singapore, the United Kingdom, Australia, Mexico, Brazil, and Japan. Locate your local office at: **international.cengage.com/region**

Cengage Learning products are represented in Canada by Nelson Education, Ltd.

For more learning solutions, please visit our corporate website at **www.cengage.com**

NOTICE TO THE READER

Printed in the United States of America
3 4 5 6 7   16 15 14 13 12

Brief Table of Contents

Table of Contents

Hacking and electronic crimes sophistication has grown at an exponential rate in recent years. In fact, recent reports have indicated that cyber crime already surpasses the illegal drug trade! Unethical hackers, better known as *black hats,* are preying on information systems of government, corporate, public, and private networks and are constantly testing the security mechanisms of these organizations to the limit with the sole aim of exploiting them and profiting from the exercise. High-profile crimes have proven that the traditional approach to computer security is simply not sufficient, even with the strongest perimeter, properly configured defense mechanisms such as firewalls, intrusion detection, and prevention systems, strong end-to-end encryption standards, and anti-virus software. Hackers have proven their dedication and ability to systematically penetrate networks all over the world. In some cases, black hats may be able to execute attacks so flawlessly that they can compromise a system, steal everything of value, and completely erase their tracks in less than 20 minutes!

The EC-Council Press is dedicated to stopping hackers in their tracks.

About EC-Council

The International Council of Electronic Commerce Consultants, better known as EC-Council, was founded in late 2001 to address the need for well-educated and certified information security and e-business practitioners. EC-Council is a global, member-based organization comprised of industry and subject matter experts all working together to set the standards and raise the bar in information security certification and education.

EC-Council first developed the *Certified Ethical Hacker* (C|EH) program. The goal of this program is to teach the methodologies, tools, and techniques used by hackers. Leveraging the collective knowledge from hundreds of subject matter experts, the C|EH program has rapidly gained popularity around the globe and is now delivered in more than 70 countries by more than 450 authorized training centers. more than 60,000 information security practitioners have been trained.

C|EH is the benchmark for many government entities and major corporations around the world. Shortly after C|EH was launched, EC-Council developed the *Certified Security Analyst* (E|CSA). The goal of the E|CSA program is to teach groundbreaking analysis methods that must be applied while conducting advanced penetration testing. The E|CSA program leads to the *Licensed Penetration Tester* (L|PT) status. The *Computer Hacking Forensic Investigator* (C|HFI) was formed with the same design methodologies and has become a global standard in certification for computer forensics. EC-Council, through its impervious network of professionals and huge industry following, has developed various other programs in information security and e-business. EC-Council certifications are viewed as the essential certifications needed when standard configuration and security policy courses fall short. Providing a true, hands-on, tactical approach to security, individuals armed with the knowledge disseminated by EC-Council programs are securing networks around the world and beating the hackers at their own game.

About the EC-Council | Press

The EC-Council | Press was formed in late 2008 as a result of a cutting-edge partnership between global information security certification leader, EC-Council and leading global academic publisher, Cengage Learning. This partnership marks a revolution in academic textbooks and courses of study in information security, computer forensics, disaster recovery, and end-user security. By identifying the essential topics and content of EC-Council professional certification programs, and repurposing this world-class content to fit academic programs, the EC-Council | Press was formed. The academic community is now able to incorporate this powerful cutting-edge content into new and existing Information Security programs. By closing the gap between academic study and professional certification, students and instructors are able to leverage the power of rigorous academic focus and high demand industry certification. The EC-Council | Press is set to revolutionize global information security programs and ultimately create a new breed of practitioners capable of combating the growing epidemic of cybercrime and the rising threat of cyber-war.

Computer Forensics Series

The EC-Council | Press Computer Forensics Series, preparing learners for C|HFI certification, is intended for those studying to become police investigators and other law enforcement personnel, defense and military personnel, e-business security professionals, systems administrators, legal professionals, banking, insurance and other professionals, government agencies, and IT managers. The content of this program is designed to expose the learner to the process of detecting attacks and collecting evidence in a forensically sound manner with the intent to report crime and prevent future attacks. Advanced techniques in computer investigation and analysis with interest in generating potential legal evidence are included. In full, this series prepares the learner to identify evidence in computer-related crime and abuse cases as well as track the intrusive hacker's path through client system.

Books in Series
- *Computer Forensics: Investigation Procedures and Response*/1435483499
- *Computer Forensics: Investigating Hard Disks, File and Operating Systems*/1435483502
- *Computer Forensics: Investigating Data and Image Files*/1435483510
- *Computer Forensics: Investigating Network Intrusions and Cybercrime*/1435483529
- *Computer Forensics: Investigating Wireless Networks and Devices*/1435483537

Investigating Wireless Networks and Devices

Investigating Wireless Networks and Devices discusses how to investigate wireless attacks, as well as PDA, iPod, iPhone, and BlackBerry forensics.

Chapter Contents

Chapter 1, *Investigating Wireless Attacks*, discusses various types of wireless technologies available, the types of attacks launched against them, and how to investigate these attacks. Chapter 2, *PDA Forensics*, provides an understanding of what is stored on PDAs and the associated security issues. It also includes a discussion on PDA forensic tools and how to implement countermeasures. Chapter 3, *iPod and iPhone Forensics*, focuses on how data stored on these devices and this data can be retrieved. Chapter 4, *BlackBerry Forensics*, discusses how the device works, ways to increase its security, and what to do if it must be taken as evidence.

Chapter Features

Many features are included in each chapter and all are designed to enhance the learner's learning experience. Features include:

- *Objectives* begin each chapter and focus the learner on the most important concepts in the chapter.

- *Key Terms* are designed to familiarize the learner with terms that will be used within the chapter.

- *Case Examples,* found throughout the chapter, present short scenarios followed by questions that challenge the learner to arrive at an answer or solution to the problem presented.

- *Chapter Summary*, at the end of each chapter, serves as a review of the key concepts covered in the chapter.

- *Review Questions* allow learners to test their comprehension of the chapter content.

- *Hands-On Projects* encourage learners to apply the knowledge they have gained after finishing the chapter. Files for the Hands-On Projects can be found on the Student Resource Center. Note: You will need your access code provided in your book to enter the site. Visit *www.cengage.com/community/eccouncil* for a link to the Student Resource Center.

Student Resource Center

The Student Resource Center contains all the files you need to complete the Hands-On Projects found at the end of the chapters. Access the Student Resource Center with the access code provided in your book. Visit *www.cengage.com/community/eccouncil* for a link to the Student Resource Center.

Additional Instructor Resources

Free to all instructors who adopt the *Investigating Wireless Networks and Devices* book for their courses is a complete package of instructor resources. These resources are available from the Course Technology Web site, *www.cengage.com/coursetechnology,* by going to the product page for this book in the online catalog, and choosing "Instructor Downloads."

Resources include:

- *Instructor Manual*: This manual includes course objectives and additional information to help your instruction.

- *ExamView Testbank*: This Windows-based testing software helps instructors design and administer tests and pre-tests. In addition to generating tests that can be printed and administered, this full-featured program has an online testing component that allows students to take tests at the computer and have their exams automatically graded.

- *PowerPoint Presentations*: This book comes with a set of Microsoft PowerPoint slides for each chapter. These slides are meant to be used as teaching aids for classroom presentations, to be made available to students for chapter review, or to be printed for classroom distribution. Instructors are also at liberty to add their own slides.

- *Labs*: These are additional hands-on activities to provide more practice for your students.

- *Assessment Activities*: These are additional assessment opportunities including discussion questions, writing assignments, Internet research activities, and homework assignments along with a final cumulative project.

- *Final Exam*: This exam provides a comprehensive assessment of *Investigating Wireless Networks and Devices* content.

Cengage Learning Information Security Community Site

Cengage Learning Information Security Community Site was created for learners and instructors to find out about the latest in information security news and technology.

Visit *community.cengage.com/infosec* to:

- Learn what's new in information security through live news feeds, videos and podcasts;

- Connect with your peers and security experts through blogs and forums;

- Browse our online catalog.

How to Become CIHFI Certified

Today's battles between corporations, governments, and countries are no longer fought only in the typical arenas of boardrooms or battlefields using physical force. Now the battlefield starts in the technical realm, which ties into most every facet of modern day life. The CIHFI certification focuses on the necessary skills to identify an intruder's footprints and to properly gather the necessary evidence to prosecute. The CIHFI certification is primarily targeted at police and other law enforcement personnel, defense and military personnel, e-business security professionals, systems administrators, legal professionals, banking, insurance and other professionals, government agencies, and IT managers. This certification will ensure that you have the knowledge and skills to identify, track, and prosecute the cyber-criminal.

CIHFI certification exams are available through authorized Prometric TESTING CENTERS. To finalize your certification after your training by taking the certification exam through a Prometric testing center, you must:

1. Apply for and purchase an exam voucher by visiting the EC-Council Press community site: *www.cengage.com/community/eccouncil,* if one was not purchased with your book.

2. Once you have your exam voucher, visit *www.prometric.com* and schedule your exam, using the information on your voucher.

CIHFI certification exams are also available through Prometric Prime. To finalize your certification after your training by taking the certification exam through Prometric Prime, you must:

1. Purchase an exam voucher by visiting the EC-Council Press community site: *www.cengage.com/community/eccouncil*, if one was not purchased with your book.

2. Speak with your instructor about scheduling an exam session, or visit the EC-Council community site referenced above for more information.

3. Take and pass the CIHFI certification examination with a score of 70% or better.

Other EC-Council I Press Products

Ethical Hacking and Countermeasures Series

The EC-Council I Press *Ethical Hacking and Countermeasures* series is intended for those studying to become security officers, auditors, security professionals, site administrators, and anyone who is concerned about or responsible for the integrity of the network infrastructure. The series includes a broad base of topics in offensive network security, ethical hacking, as well as network defense and countermeasures. The content of this series is designed to immerse learners into an interactive environment where they will be shown how to scan, test, hack, and secure information systems. A wide variety of tools, viruses, and malware is presented in these books, providing a complete understanding of the tactics and tools used by hackers. By gaining a thorough understanding of how hackers operate, ethical hackers are able to set up strong countermeasures and defensive systems to protect their organization's critical infrastructure and information. The series, when used in its entirety, helps prepare readers to take and succeed on the CIEH certification exam from EC-Council.

Books in Series
- *Ethical Hacking and Countermeasures: Attack Phases*/143548360X
- *Ethical Hacking and Countermeasures: Threats and Defense Mechanisms*/1435483618
- *Ethical Hacking and Countermeasures: Web Applications and Data Servers*/1435483626
- *Ethical Hacking and Countermeasures: Linux, Macintosh and Mobile Systems*/1435483642
- *Ethical Hacking and Countermeasures: Secure Network Infrastructures*/1435483650

Network Security Administrator Series

The EC-Council I Press *Network Administrator* series, preparing learners for EINSA certification, is intended for those studying to become system administrators, network administrators and anyone who is interested in network security technologies. This series is designed to educate learners, from a vendor neutral standpoint, how to defend the networks they manage. This series covers the fundamental skills in evaluating internal and external threats to network security, design, and how to enforce network level security policies, and ultimately protect an organization's information. Covering a broad range of topics from secure network fundamentals, protocols and analysis, standards and policy, hardening infrastructure, to configuring IPS, IDS and firewalls, bastion host and honeypots, among many other topics, learners completing this series will have a full understanding of defensive measures taken to secure their organizations' information. The series, when used in its entirety, helps prepare readers to take and succeed on the EINSA, Network Security Administrator certification exam from EC-Council.

Books in Series
- *Network Defense: Fundamentals and Protocols*/1435483553
- *Network Defense: Security Policy and Threats*/1435483561
- *Network Defense: Perimeter Defense Mechanisms*/143548357X
- *Network Defense: Securing and Troubleshooting Network Operating Systems*/1435483588
- *Network Defense: Security and Vulnerability Assessment*/1435483596

Security Analyst Series

The EC-Council I Press *Penetration Testing* series, preparing learners for EICSA/LPT certification, is intended for those studying to become network server administrators, firewall administrators, security testers, system administrators and risk assessment professionals. This series covers a broad base of topics in advanced penetration testing and security analysis. The content of this program is designed to expose the learner to groundbreaking methodologies in conducting thorough security analysis, as well as advanced penetration testing techniques. Armed with the knowledge from the *Penetration Testing* series, learners will be able to perform the intensive assessments required to effectively identify and mitigate risks to the security of the organizations infrastructure. The series, when used in its entirety, helps prepare readers to take and succeed on the E|CSA, Certified Security Analyst, and L|PT, License Penetration Tester certification exam from EC-Council.

Books in Series
- *Penetration Testing: Security Analysis*/1435483669
- *Penetration Testing: Procedures and Methodologies Analysis*/1435483677
- *Penetration Testing: Network and Perimeter Testing*/1435483685
- *Penetration Testing: Communication Media Testing Analysis*/1435483693
- *Penetration Testing: Network Threat Testing*/1435483707

Cyber Safety/1435483715

Cyber Safety is designed for anyone who is interested in learning computer networking and security basics. This product provides information cyber crime; security procedures; how to recognize security threats and attacks, incident response, and how to secure Internet access. This book gives individuals the basic security literacy skills to begin high-end IT programs. The book also prepares readers to take and succeed on the Security|5 certification exam from EC-Council.

Wireless Safety/1435483766

Wireless Safety introduces the learner to the basics of wireless technologies and its practical adaptation. *Wireless|5* is tailored to cater to any individual's desire to learn more about wireless technology. It requires no pre-requisite knowledge and aims to educate the learner in simple applications of these technologies. Topics include wireless signal propagation, IEEE and ETSI wireless standards, WLANs and operation, wireless protocols and communication languages, wireless devices, and wireless security networks. The book also prepares readers to take and succeed on the Wireless|5 certification exam from EC-Council.

Network Safety/1435483774

Network Safety provides the basic core knowledge on how infrastructure enables a working environment. It is intended for those in office environments and home users who wants to optimize resource utilization, share infrastructure, and make the best of technology and the convenience it offers. Topics include foundations of networks, networking components, wireless networks, basic hardware components, the networking environment and connectivity as well as troubleshooting. The book also prepares readers to take and succeed on the Network|5 certification exam from EC-Council.

Disaster Recovery Series

The *Disaster Recovery Series* is designed to fortify virtualization technology knowledge of system administrators, systems engineers, enterprise system architects, and any IT professional who is concerned about the integrity of their network infrastructure. Virtualization technology gives the advantage of additional flexibility as well as cost savings while deploying a disaster recovery solution. The series when used in its entirety helps prepare readers to take and succeed on the E|CDR and E|CVT, Disaster Recovery and Virtualization Technology certification exam from EC-Council. The EC-Council Certified Disaster Recovery and Virtualization Technology professional will have a better understanding of how to setup Disaster Recovery Plans using traditional and virtual technologies to ensure business continuity in the event of a disaster.

Books in Series
- *Disaster Recovery*/1435488709
- *Virtualization Security*/1435488695

Acknowledgements

Michael H. Goldner is the Chair of the School of Information Technology for ITT Technical Institute in Norfolk Virginia, and also teaches bachelor level courses in computer network and information security systems. Michael has served on and chaired ITT Educational Services Inc. National Curriculum Committee on Information Security. He received his Juris Doctorate from Stetson University College of Law, his undergraduate degree from Miami University and has been working for more than 15 years in the area of information technology. He is an active member of the American Bar Association, and has served on that organization's cyber law committee. He is a member of IEEE, ACM, and ISSA, and is the holder of a number of industrially recognized certifications including, CISSP, CEH, CHFI, CEI, MCT, MCSE/Security, Security +, Network +, and A+. Michael recently completed the design and creation of a computer forensic program for ITT Technical Institute, and has worked closely with both EC-Council and Delmar/Cengage Learning in the creation of this EC-Council Press series.

Chapter 1

Investigating Wireless Attacks

Objectives

After completing this chapter, you should be able to:

- Understand wireless networking technologies
- Describe wireless attacks
- Hijack and modify a wireless network
- Describe the association of a wireless access point (WAP) and a device
- Perform network forensics in a wireless environment
- Enumerate the steps for investigating a wireless attack
- Describe active and passive wireless scanning techniques
- Describe the tools used to investigate wireless attacks
- Describe rogue access points and the tools used to detect them

Key Terms

Active attack a type of attack in which an attacker tries to alter or corrupt the data or services on a network

Passive attack a type of attack where an unauthorized user monitors communications to gather information

Warchalking a technique involving using chalk to place a special symbol on a sidewalk or another surface to indicate a nearby wireless network that offers Internet access

Wardriving a technique hackers use to locate insecure wireless networks while driving around

Warflying a technique hackers use to locate insecure wireless networks while flying around

Introduction to Investigating Wireless Attacks

This chapter focuses on investigating wireless attacks. It discusses the various types of wireless technologies available and the different types of attacks launched against them. It also covers how to investigate a wireless attack.

Wireless Networking Technologies

The growth of wireless networking technology has given rise to many security issues. Wireless technology has become popular because of its convenience and low cost. A wireless local area network (WLAN) allows workers to access digital resources without being tied to their desks. It is often cheaper and easier to set up a wireless network than to run cables throughout an organization's facilities. The following are some of the more prominent wireless networking technologies:

- Bluetooth
- Infrared
- Ultrawideband
- ZigBee
- Wireless USB
- Wi-Fi
- WiMAX
- Satellite

Wireless Attacks

There are various kinds of wireless attacks. The following are some methods hackers use to facilitate wireless attacks:

- *Wardriving*: *Wardriving* is a technique hackers use to locate insecure wireless networks while driving around.
- *Warflying*: Similar to wardriving, **warflying** involves flying around in an aircraft, looking for open wireless networks.
- *Warchalking*: **Warchalking** involves using chalk to place a special symbol on a sidewalk or another surface to indicate a nearby wireless network that offers Internet access.

Passive Attacks

A *passive attack* is a type of attack where an unauthorized user monitors communications to gather information. For example, eavesdropping on network traffic is a passive attack. An eavesdropper can easily seize the network traffic using tools such as Network Monitor, Tcpdump, or AirSnort.

Passive attacks are difficult to detect and identify. Passive attacks are often symmetric, meaning that the attacker can monitor the communication in both directions. Some other examples of passive attacks are traffic analysis and traffic monitoring.

Electronic Emanations

Electronic emanations are the electromagnetic waves of radiation that electronic devices emit during their operation. Wireless technology is subject to these emanations. An attacker can intercept the emanations and use them to figure out how to gain the proper credentials to join a wireless network. The major problem is that the administrator of the network cannot identify that the attacker has intercepted the signals.

Active Attacks

Active attacks on wireless networks are similar to those on wired networks, in which an attacker tries to alter or corrupt the data or services on a network. These types of attacks include flooding, spoofing, and unauthorized access. The information that an attacker collects during a successful passive attack can make it easier for him or her to actively attack a network.

Denial-Of-Service Attacks

Wireless systems are vulnerable to the same protocol-based DoS attacks that strike wired networks. They are also vulnerable to other types of DoS attacks, because the signals used to transmit data over the air can be easily disrupted. The main objective of DoS attacks is to deny access to network services and resources. It is difficult to track such attacks on wireless networks.

Modes of Attack DoS attacks have varied modes of attacks that include consumption, alteration, and physical destruction of network components or resources. The following are some common modes of attack:

- *Consumption of resources*: This involves consuming the resources a system needs, including the following:
  - *Bandwidth*: An intruder can redirect packets to the network in order to consume all of the available bandwidth on the network.
  - *Memory*: This is normally accomplished by saving unnecessary e-mails, causing intentional errors, or sharing unimportant files and folders.
- *Alteration of resources or information*: Altering the configuration of a machine can prevent a user from being able to use it.
- *Physical destruction of the computer/network elements*: This type of attack concerns the destruction of the physical elements, such as computers and routers.

Results of DoS Attacks The most significant loss due to these attacks is the time and money that an organization loses while the services are unavailable.

Flooding

The goal of flooding is to degrade the performance of the network by directing unnecessary packets of data toward it. This may result in a loss of connection requests or a complete denial of service. Flooding is a multicasting technique wherein packets from one source are directed toward multiple destinations on the network.

Man-In-The-Middle Attack

A man-in-the middle (MITM) attack is when an intruder accesses information being transmitted between the sender and the receiver. The transmission proves to be insecure because the information is not encrypted. In such cases, there is a possibility of the intruder altering the data.

The following are the two types of MITM attacks:

1. *Eavesdropping*: Eavesdropping is a passive attack technique. The attacker intercepts data being transmitted between one system and another. Security mechanisms such as IPSec, SSH, and SSL help prevent eavesdropping.
2. *Manipulation*: Manipulation is an extended step of eavesdropping. In this type of man-in-the-middle attack, the attacker manipulates the data that he or she intercepts. This manipulation can be done using a technique such as ARP poisoning.

Hijacking and Modifying a Wireless Network

In a wireless network, TCP/IP packets go through switches, routers, and wireless access points. Each device looks at the destination IP address and checks for that address in its table of local IP addresses. This table is dynamically built up from traffic that passes through the device and from Address Resolution Protocol (ARP) notifications from devices joining the network. If the destination IP address is not in the device's table, it passes the address off to its default gateway.

However, there is no authentication or verification of the validity of a packet that a device receives. A malicious user can send messages to routing devices and access points stating that his or her MAC address is associated with a known IP address. All traffic that goes through those devices that is intended for the hijacked IP address will instead go to the malicious user's machine.

Association of a Wireless Access Point and a Device

A wireless access point (WAP) is a node configured to allow wireless devices to access the local area network (LAN). WAPs are just plugged into a switch or into an Ethernet hub. An access point has its own range. When two or more access points are in an environment, the range overlaps to provide roaming. The following two methods provide some level of security between a device and the WAP with which it is associated:

1. *MAC filtering*: The media access control (MAC) address is the 12-character (48 bits written in hexadecimal notation) unique hardware address of a particular system. The MAC address is used in the data-link layer of the network. MAC filtering is used to restrict unauthorized users. Only those devices with MAC addresses on the WAP's white list are allowed access to the network.

2. *Preshared key (PSK) or use of encryption*: The wireless device and the access point use a shared secret key. A checksum is added to every packet transmitted over the network. If the packet is cracked, then the value of the checksum changes, and it is easy to identify the intrusion. The transmitting device creates a packet-concentrated vector that is combined with the key to encrypt the packet. At the receiving end, the same key is used to decrypt the packet.

Network Forensics in a Wireless Environment

The following are the steps involved in performing forensic investigations in a wireless environment:

1. Obtain a search warrant.
2. Identify wireless devices.
3. Document the scene and maintain the chain of custody.
4. Detect wireless connections.
5. Determine the wireless field's strength.
6. Map wireless zones and hot spots.
7. Connect to the wireless network.
8. Acquire and analyze wireless data.
9. Generate a report.

Obtain a Search Warrant

The investigator should ensure that the search warrant application addresses the on-site examination of all computers and wireless-related equipment. The investigator can perform forensic analysis only on those pieces of equipment specified in the warrant. He or she should be careful not to overlook wireless devices that are in range of a WAP but may not be in the same room.

Identify Wireless Devices

The investigator needs to identify all the different wireless devices connected to the network. He or she needs to check the physical locations of the following wireless hardware:

- Wireless routers
- Wireless access points
- Wireless modems
- Wireless network adapters
- Repeaters
- Hard drives
- Antennas

Searching for Additional Devices

To find additional wireless devices on the network that may not be readily apparent, the investigator can put his or her forensic laptop in promiscuous mode and send deauthentication packets using the Aireplay tool. This may force the active wireless equipment to reconnect to the default wireless access point, which will be redirected to the forensic laptop (since the laptop is running in promiscuous mode). Aireplay is a wireless assessment tool that injects specially crafted data packets into a wireless stream.

Detecting Wireless Access Points (WAPs)

The investigator can use the following techniques to find WAPs:

- *Manual detection*: For manual detection, the investigator has to configure some sort of mobile device such as a handheld PC or laptop. To detect WAPs, the investigator has to physically visit the area where a WAP is likely to be. He or she can then use techniques such as wardriving or warflying to detect the WAPs.

- *Active wireless scanning technique*: The active scanning technique involves broadcasting a probe message and waiting for a response from devices in the range. This technique identifies many WAPs but obviously cannot find those WAPs that do not respond to the probe message.

- *Passive wireless scanning technique*: The passive scanning technique identifies the presence of any wireless communication. Through this technique, an investigator can identify all active WAP connections, but he or she may not find a WAP that is not currently serving any devices.

- *Nessus vulnerability scanner*: The investigator can use Nessus to find WAPs by performing the following steps:

  - Update plug-in #11026 with the nessus-update-plugins command.

  - Choose plug-in #11026 in the General family of scans.

  - Enable a port scan for ports 1–100.

  - Disable the **Safe Checks** option.

  - Enable the **Enable Dependencies at Runtime** option.

Rogue Access Point

A rogue access point is an unauthorized access point in a wireless network. Attackers typically deploy these access points to sniff important data on the network. Attackers can also use rogue access points to hijack user sessions on the wireless network.

An investigator can detect a rogue access point by following two steps:

1. *Access point detection*: The investigator first needs to use one of the techniques for detecting a wireless access point to discover the access point on the network.

2. *Verifying whether or not the access point is a rogue access point*: After identifying the access point in the network, the next step is to verify whether or not the identified access point is a rogue access point. To tell whether an access point is authorized, the investigator has to check the following:

   - MAC
   - SSID
   - Vendor
   - Media type
   - Channel

Tools for Detecting Rogue Access Points

Network Stumbler and MiniStumbler are other tools that help investigators discover rogue access points.

Network Stumbler Network Stumbler (Figure 1-1) is a Windows utility that is often used for wardriving. It is a high-level WLAN scanner that operates by sending a steady stream of broadcast packets on all possible channels. Access points respond to the broadcast packets to verify their existence, even if beacons have been disabled.

Network Stumbler displays information about the access point, including the following:

- Signal-to-noise ratio
- MAC address
- SSID
- Channel details

A user can also connect to a GPS to find location information about any access points discovered.

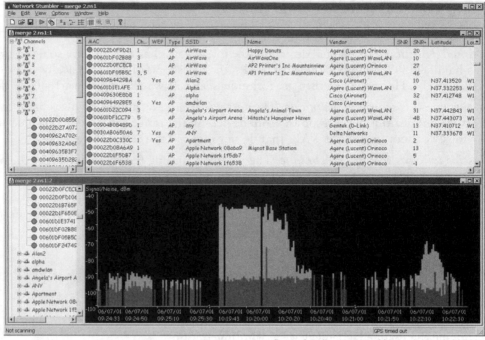

Figure 1-1   Network Stumbler displays information about the access points it discovers.

MiniStumbler   MiniStumbler is the smaller sibling of Network Stumbler. It provides much of the same information as Network Stumbler, but is written for handheld devices running Pocket PC or Windows Mobile operating systems. Figure 1-2 shows a screenshot from MiniStumbler.

Document the Scene and Maintain the Chain of Custody

The investigator should do the following at the scene:

- Document all devices connected to the wireless network
- Take photographs of all evidence
- Document the state of each device during seizure
- Maintain the chain of custody of documents, photographs, and evidence

Detect Wireless Connections

The investigator can detect wireless connection using scanning tools such as the following:

- ClassicStumbler
- MacStumbler
- iStumbler
- Airport Signal
- Airfart
- Kismet

ClassicStumbler

ClassicStumbler scans for WAPs and displays information about each WAP within range. The information it displays includes the following:

- Signal strength
- Noise strength

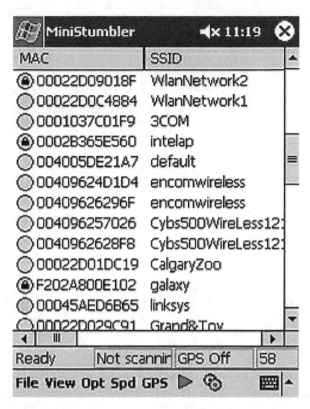

Figure 1-2 MiniStumbler is a version of Network Stumbler for handheld devices.

- Network type
- Channel

Figure 1-3 shows a screenshot from ClassicStumbler.

MacStumbler

MacStumbler displays information about nearby 802.11b and 802.11g wireless access points. It helps an investigator find access points in the field or to diagnose wireless network problems. MacStumbler requires an Apple Airport Card and Mac OS 10.1 or later. Figure 1-4 shows a screenshot from MacStumbler.

iStumbler

iStumbler is a wireless tool for Mac OS X that provides plug-ins for finding and discovering information about AirPort networks, Bluetooth devices, and Bonjour services. The Spectrum Widget included with iStumbler displays a virtual spectrum analyzer on the Dashboard, allowing a user to visually detect network radio frequency overlap. Figure 1-5 shows a screenshot from iStumbler.

AirPort Signal

The AirPort Signal tool scans for open networks within range. It creates a table row for each station detected, with information about the signals it received.

The following are some of the features of AirPort Signal:

- Reports signal usability as signal-to-noise ratio in dB.
- Supports directed scanning to monitor closed networks or to specify a network of interest. AirPort Signal can merge signals from multiple stations on the same network.

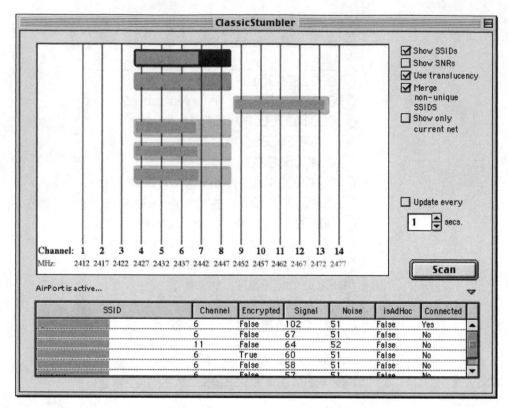

Figure 1-3 ClassicStumbler scans for WAPs within range.

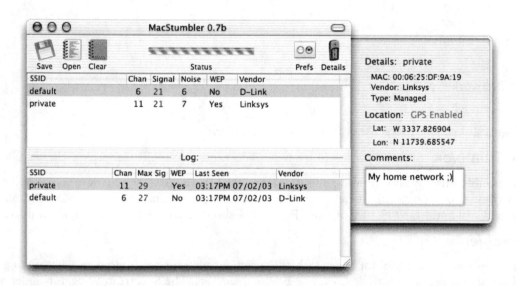

Figure 1-4 MacStumbler displays important information about each WAP it finds.

- Displays a full history of previous scans for comparing performance.
- Allows users to annotate, save, and restore previous scan results.

Figure 1-6 shows a screenshot from AirPort Signal.

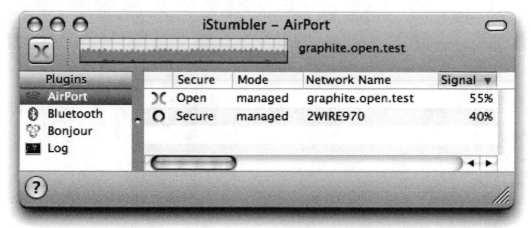

Figure 1-5   iStumbler detects AirPort networks, Bluetooth devices, and Bonjour services.

Time	Network Name	Chan	Type	Signal	Noise	SNR dB	SNR plot	Notes
2004-07-06 10:31:06	Sustworks	11	AP WEP	59	21	38	●●●●●●●●●●●●●	Tx Rate=11
2004-07-06 10:31:00	Sustworks	11	AP WEP	59	22	37	●●●●●●●●●●●●	Tx Rate=11

Network Name: Sustworks ▾   ☐ Merge Similar Names   Limit: 2   Delay: 5

(?) Scan OK   (Delete) (Scan)

Figure 1-6   AirPort Signal scans for wireless networks in the area.

Airfart

Airfart detects wireless devices and calculates their signal strength. It implements a modular n-tier architecture with data collection at the bottom tier and a graphical user interface at the top. Figure 1-7 shows a screenshot from Airfart.

Kismet

Kismet is completely passive and is capable of detecting traffic from WAPs and wireless clients. It works on both open and closed networks. It requires an 802.11b network card capable of entering RF monitoring mode. Once in RF monitoring mode, the card is no longer able to associate with a wireless network. Kismet needs to run as root, but it can switch to a UID with lower privileges as it begins to capture. Figure 1-8 shows a screenshot from Kismet.

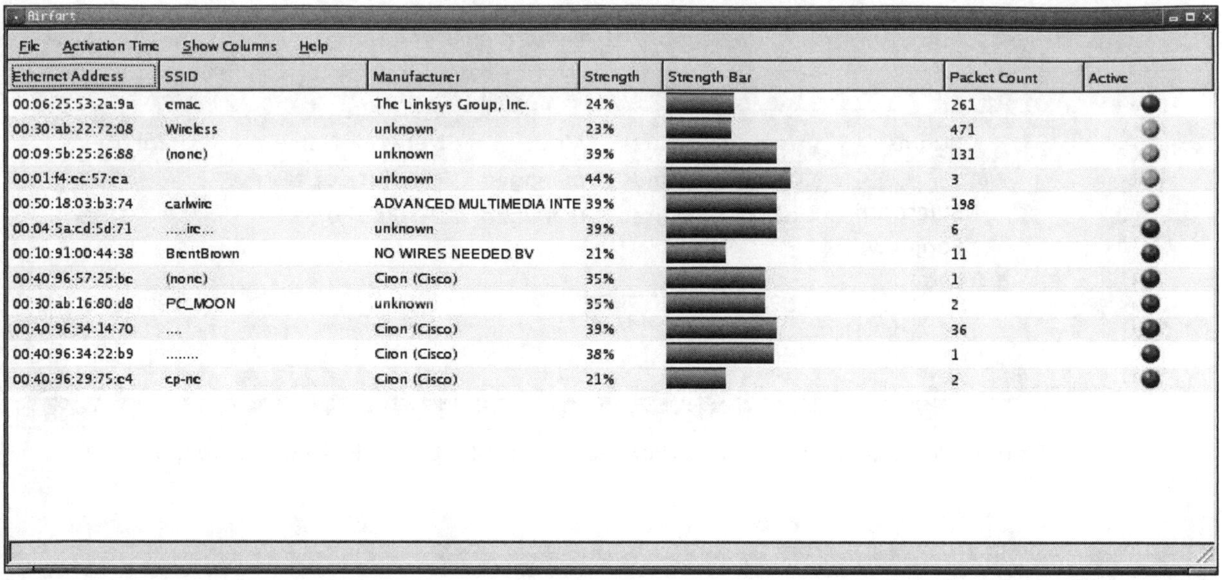

Source: http://nixbit.com/. Accessed 2/2007.

Figure 1-7   Airfart shows the signal strength of the wireless devices it detects.

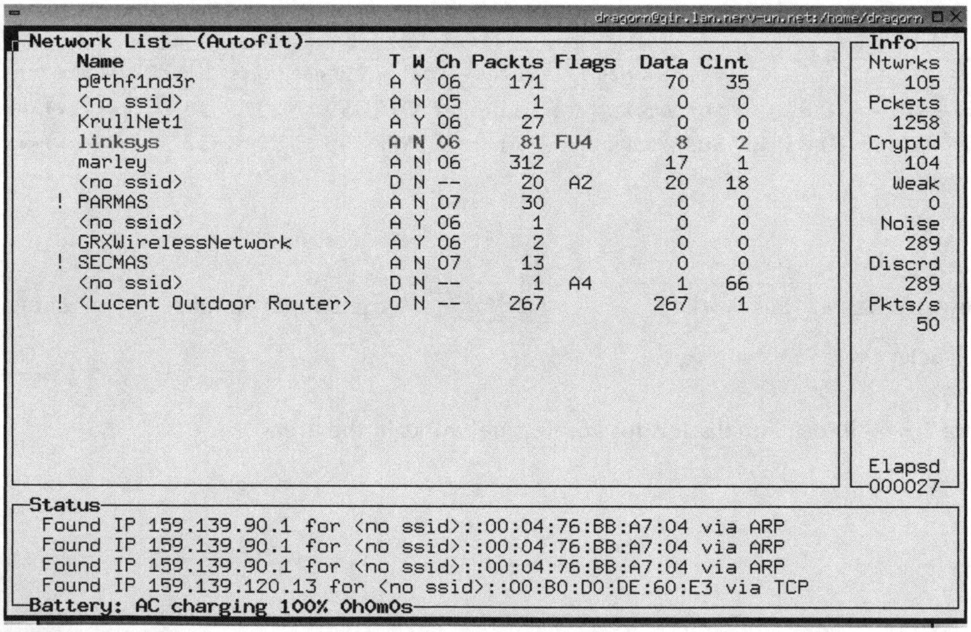

Source: http://www.kismetwireless.net/. Accessed 2/2007.

Figure 1-8   Kismet detects traffic from wireless devices.

Determine the Wireless Field's Strength

The investigator can use a tool called Field Strength Meter (FSM) to determine the wireless field's strength. FSM is a software application that extends a conventional SSB receiver to allow an investigator to measure and calculate the field strength of radio signals or interference.

The following are some of the features of FSM:

- Measures true root-mean-square (RMS), quasipeak, and peak audio power
- Calculates received RF power (RMS, quasipeak, and peak) in dBm
- Calculates field strength (RMS, quasipeak, and peak) in dBuV/m

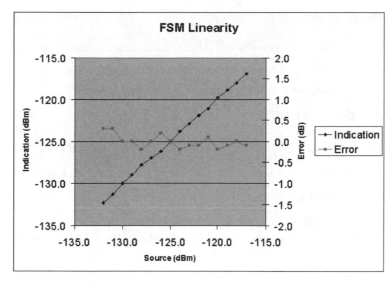

Figure 1-9 FSM measures different aspects of the wireless field.

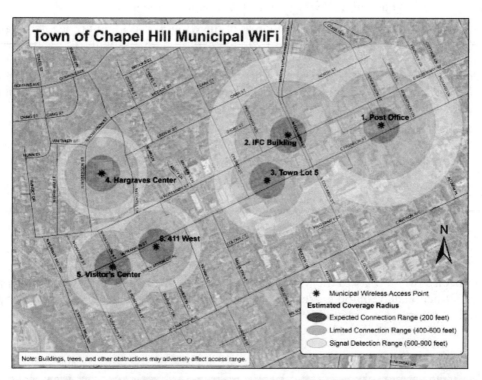

Figure 1-10   An investigator can use the data he or she has gathered to create a map of wireless zones and hot spots.

- Extrapolates calculated field strengths to a normalized bandwidth for comparisons
- Saves results to text files, e-mails, and Web transactions

Figure 1-9 shows a screenshot from FSM.

Map Wireless Zones and Hot Spots

Once an investigator has detected all wireless connections and collected other information about the wireless networks involved in the crime, he or she can analyze all the information to prepare a static map of the wireless zones and hot spots. Investigators typically use tools such as Microsoft Visio to create these maps. Figure 1-10 shows a map of wireless zones and hot spots.

Connect to the Wireless Network

The following are methods for accessing a WAP:

- Directly connecting to the wireless access point
- Sniffing traffic between the access point and associated devices

Directly Connecting to the Wireless Access Point

To directly connect to the WAP, the investigator needs a network cable, a forensic laptop, and the wireless access point. The forensic laptop should have a standard network adapter.

The investigator can take the following steps to connect to the wireless access point:

1. Use the network cable to connect the laptop and wireless access point.

2. Determine whether the laptop has to be assigned an IP address.

   a. If the wireless access point and laptop have DHCP enabled, then the laptop will automatically be assigned an IP.

   b. If DHCP is not enabled on the WAP, the investigator will need to assign an IP address to the forensic laptop that is in the same class as the wireless access point. The IP address of the wireless access point can be determined by typing the command ipconfig in the command prompt. This displays the IP address of the default gateway (Figure 1-11), which is the wireless access point.

3. Once the investigator gets the IP address of the wireless access point, he or she can try connecting to the WAP using a Web browser. A login window will pop up and will ask the investigator to fill in the credentials for obtaining access to the wireless access point. Often, users don't change the default username and password for wireless access points. An investigator can go to *http://www.governmentsecurity.org/ default_logins_and_passwords_for_networked_devices* to find the default usernames and passwords for many popular network devices. Figure 1-12 shows this Web site.

4. When successfully logged in to the wireless access point, the investigator will see a screen similar to the one shown in Figure 1-13, which shows the browser interface for Netgear's WGR614 wireless router. The investigator can collect and store a wealth of information about the wireless network.

5. Click on **Attached Devices** to find all of the devices connected to the wireless access point. Record all information about each device, including IP address, device name, and MAC address. Figure 1-14 shows this screen.

6. Click on **LAN IP Setup** to find the LAN TCP/IP setup, as shown in Figure 1-15.

7. Click on other menu items to find any information relevant to the case.

If connected over a LAN to the wireless access point, a ping sweep can reveal other connected systems on the network. Other related computers should also respond to this ping request if they are not protected by a firewall. The investigator can use a tool like Nmap to perform a ping sweep and other functions related to scanning.

```
C:\>ipconfig

Windows IP Configuration


Ethernet adapter Local Area Connection:

        Connection-specific DNS Suffix   . :
        IP Address. . . . . . . . . . . . : 10.0.0.253
        Subnet Mask . . . . . . . . . . . : 255.255.255.0
        Default Gateway . . . . . . . . . : 10.0.0.1

C:\>_
```

Figure 1-11   The default gateway address is the address of the WAP.

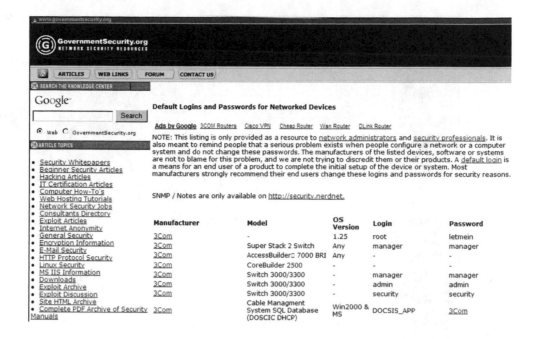

Figure 1-12   An investigator can easily find the default usernames and passwords for wireless devices.

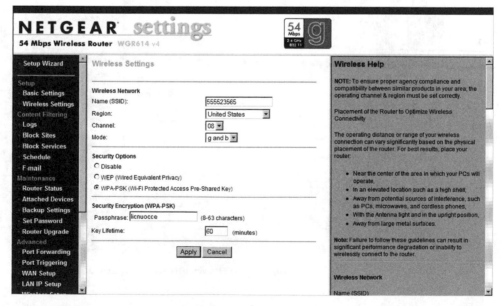

Figure 1-13   An investigator can discover information about the wireless network by logging in to the WAP's browser interface.

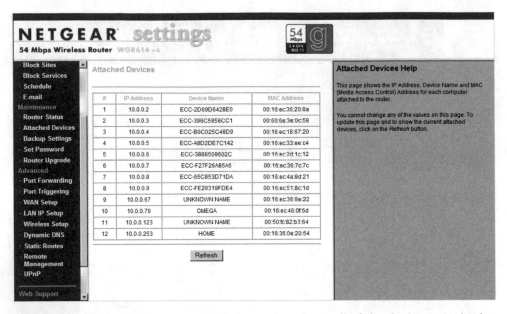

Figure 1-14 An investigator can see information about all of the devices attached to the WAP.

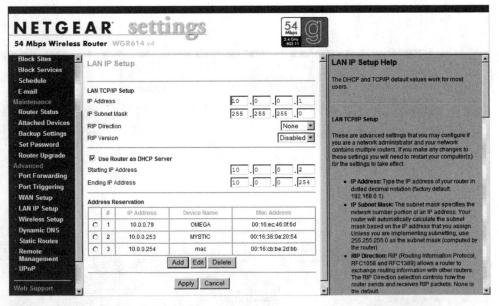

Figure 1-15 The **LAN IP Setup** screen shows information about the WAP's TCP/IP setup.

Using Nmap to Scan Wireless Access Points An investigator can find live hosts on the network by using Nmap. For example, the command **nmap -sP -v 10.0.0.1/24** will show all the live hosts on the same subnet. Nmap will display the vendor and MAC address information on the screen. To find more information about a specific address—10.0.0.1, for example—the investigator can run the command **nmap -sS -A 10.0.0.1**. If the investigator wants to view information about an entire network subnet, then he or she can run the command **nmap -sS -A 192.168.5.0/24**.

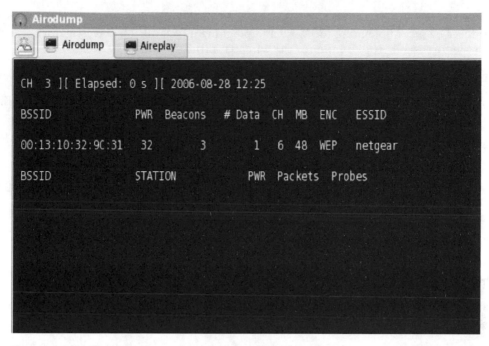

Figure 1-16   Airodump scans for wireless access points.

Sniffing Traffic Between the Access Point and Associated Devices

For this technique, the forensic laptop is placed in promiscuous mode and sniffs all traffic between the access point and its associated devices. The investigator can use the BackTrack tool to find devices connected to the wireless network. The Aircrack suite in BackTrack includes two programs: Airodump and Aireplay.

Scanning Using Airodump   Airodump scans all wireless channels, searching for access points. Figure 1-16 shows Airodump performing a scan.

Airodump displays the following information about each access point it finds:

- BSSID: MAC address of the access point
- PWR: Relative strength of wireless signal
- Beacons: Number of beacon packets received
- # Data: Number of packets that can be decrypted
- CH: Channel the access point is transmitting on
- MB: Current rate of data transfer in megabits per second
- ENC: Encryption level set on the access point
- ESSID: SSID of the device

Columns BSSID, CH, and ESSID contain important information that will be useful during the initial phase of the scan. Airodump needs to capture a number of packets to determine the type of encryption used.

Using Aireplay to Force Associated Devices to Reconnect   The Aireplay tool attempts to confuse the connected wireless devices by sending deauthentication packets. The wireless devices are made to think that the wireless access point is not functioning. Once disconnected, the devices attempt to reconnect to the same access point. Airodump should be running in the background while the deauthentication packets are sent. An investigator can use the following command to send the deauthentication packets:

aireplay-ng --deauth 5 -a <MAC of WAP> <interface>

The interface in this command specifies the type of the wireless network card on the forensic laptop.

If physical access to the wireless access point is available, then the investigator can force the associated devices to reconnect by just unplugging the WAP and plugging it back in. The investigator should have Airodump running on the forensic laptop to monitor the wireless traffic.

Acquire and Analyze Data

The investigator can capture wireless traffic using wireless network monitoring and sniffing tools such as Wireshark and Tcpdump.

Wireshark

Wireshark is a free network protocol analyzer for UNIX, Linux, Mac OS X, and Windows. It allows the investigator to examine data from a live network or from a capture file on disk. The investigator can see all traffic being passed over the network by putting the network interface into promiscuous mode.

The following are some of the features of Wireshark:

- Capture data can be browsed via GUI or the command line.
- Capture files can be programmatically edited.
- Display filters can be used to selectively highlight and color packet summary information.
- Hundreds of protocols can be dissected.

Figure 1-17 shows a screenshot from Wireshark.

Tcpdump

Tcpdump is a command-line network-debugging tool. It allows the investigator to intercept and display TCP/IP and other packets being transmitted or received over the network to which the investigator's computer is attached.

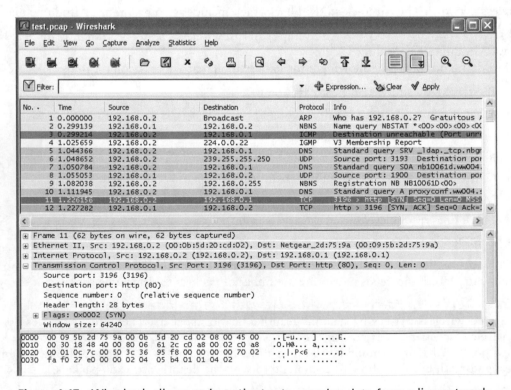

Figure 1-17 Wireshark allows an investigator to examine data from a live network.

Tcpdump Commands   The following are some examples of Tcpdump commands:

- Exporting Tcpdump output to a file:
  - **tcpdump port 80 -l > webdump.txt & tail -f webdump.txt**
  - **tcpdump -w rawdump**
  - **tcpdump -r rawdump > rawdump.txt**
  - **tcpdump -c1000 -w rawdump**
  - **tcpdump -i eth1 -c1000 -w rawdump**
- Capturing traffic on a specific port:
  - **tcpdump port 80**
- Capturing traffic that passes between specific hosts on the LAN:
  - **tcpdump host workstation4 and workstation11 and workstation13**
- Capturing all packets except those for certain ports:
  - **tcpdump not port 110 and not port 25 and not port 53 and not port 22**
- Filtering by protocol:
  - **tcpdump udp**
  - **tcpdump ip proto OSPFIGP**
- Capturing traffic on a specific host and restricting by protocol:
  - **tcpdump host server02 and ip**
  - **tcpdump host server03 and not udp**
  - **tcpdump host server03 and ip and igmp and not udp**

Figure 1-18 shows a screenshot from Tcpdump.

Acquiring Other Data and Performing Analysis

The investigator should acquire the DHCP logs, firewall logs, and network logs. He or she can use tools like fwanalog and Firewall Analyzer to view the firewall log files. The investigator should check the following:

- DHCP log files for issued IP addresses (Figure 1-19)
- Firewall log files for intrusions
- Network log files for intrusion activities

The investigator can use tools like Hydra and Cain & Abel to crack the passwords on password-protected log files. The investigator should also analyze the registry on any Windows computers for information about any wireless devices the computer has used.

```
13:57:08.461444 DORIS.SLAC.Stanford.EDU.22648 > www.cern.ch.http: S 1412042008:1412042008(0) win 512 <mss 1460>
13:57:08.681444 www.cern.ch.http > DORIS.SLAC.Stanford.EDU.22648: S 3576032358:3576032358(0) ack 1412042009 win 8760 <mss 1460> (DF)
13:57:08.681444 DORIS.SLAC.Stanford.EDU.22648 > www.cern.ch.http: . ack 1 win 32120 (DF)
13:57:08.681444 DORIS.SLAC.Stanford.EDU.22648 > www.cern.ch.http: P 1:701(700) ack 1 win 32120 (DF)
13:57:08.901444 www.cern.ch.http > DORIS.SLAC.Stanford.EDU.22648: . ack 701 win 8760 (DF)
13:57:08.911444 www.cern.ch.http > DORIS.SLAC.Stanford.EDU.22648: P 1:1461(1460) ack 701 win 8760 (DF)
13:57:08.931444 DORIS.SLAC.Stanford.EDU.22648 > www.cern.ch.http: . ack 1461 win 32120 (DF)
13:57:09.151444 www.cern.ch.http > DORIS.SLAC.Stanford.EDU.22648: . 1461:2921(1460) ack 701 win 8760 (DF)
13:57:09.151444 www.cern.ch.http > DORIS.SLAC.Stanford.EDU.22648: P 2921:4381(1460) ack 701 win 8760 (DF)
13:57:09.161444 DORIS.SLAC.Stanford.EDU.22648 > www.cern.ch.http: . ack 4381 win 30660 (DF)
13:57:09.381444 www.cern.ch.http > DORIS.SLAC.Stanford.EDU.22648: . 4381:5231(850) ack 701 win 8760 (DF)
13:57:09.381444 www.cern.ch.http > DORIS.SLAC.Stanford.EDU.22648: . 5231:6691(1460) ack 701 win 8760 (DF)
13:57:09.381444 www.cern.ch.http > DORIS.SLAC.Stanford.EDU.22648: . 6691:8151(1460) ack 701 win 8760 (DF)
13:57:09.391444 DORIS.SLAC.Stanford.EDU.22648 > www.cern.ch.http: . ack 8151 win 29200 (DF)
13:57:09.611444 www.cern.ch.http > DORIS.SLAC.Stanford.EDU.22648: . 8151:9327(1176) ack 701 win 8760 (DF)
13:57:09.611444 www.cern.ch.http > DORIS.SLAC.Stanford.EDU.22648: . 9327:10787(1460) ack 701 win 8760 (DF)
13:57:09.611444 www.cern.ch.http > DORIS.SLAC.Stanford.EDU.22648: P 10787:12247(1460) ack 701 win 8760 (DF)
13:57:09.611444 www.cern.ch.http > DORIS.SLAC.Stanford.EDU.22648: P 12247:13058(811) ack 701 win 8760 (DF)
13:57:09.611444 www.cern.ch.http > DORIS.SLAC.Stanford.EDU.22648: F 13058:13058(0) ack 701 win 8760 (DF)
13:57:09.611444 DORIS.SLAC.Stanford.EDU.22648 > www.cern.ch.http: . ack 13059 win 24820 (DF)
13:57:11.171444 DORIS.SLAC.Stanford.EDU.22648 > www.cern.ch.http: F 701:701(0) ack 13059 win 32120
13:57:11.391444 www.cern.ch.http > DORIS.SLAC.Stanford.EDU.22648: . ack 702 win 8760 (DF)
```

Figure 1-18   Tcpdump intercepts packets on the network and displays information about each one.

ID	Date	Time	Description	IP Address	Host Name	Mac Address
11	8/24/00	00:00:58	Renew	xxx.xxx.xx.xxx	Acme.*domain*.com	00xxxxxxxxxx
11	8/24/00	00:03:28	Renew	xxx.xxx.xx.xxx	Acme.*domain*.com	00xxxxxxxxxx
11	8/24/00	00:05:58	Renew	xxx.xxx.xx.xxx	Acme.*domain*.com	00xxxxxxxxxx

Figure 1-19   The investigator can look at the DHCP logs to find what IP addresses were issued to what MAC addresses.

Generate a Report

The investigator's report should include the following:

- Name of the investigator
- List of wireless evidence
- Documents of the evidence and other supporting items
- List of tools used for investigation
- Devices and setup used in the examination
- Brief description of the examination steps
- Details about the findings:
  - Information about the files
  - Internet-related evidence
  - Data and image analysis
- Investigator's conclusion

Chapter Summary

- Security between a wireless access point and its associated devices is provided through either MAC filtering or the use of a preshared key (PSK) or encryption.
- Methods to access a wireless access point include directly connecting to the WAP and sniffing traffic between the access point and associated devices.
- A rogue access point is one that is not authorized for operation on a network.
- In the active scanning technique, a scanner broadcasts a probe message and waits for a response from devices within range.
- The passive scanning technique detects all active WAP connections but may not find a WAP that is not currently serving any devices.
- To investigate wireless attacks, an investigator needs to check DHCP log files for issued IP addresses, firewall log files for intrusions, and network log files for intrusion activities.

Review Questions

1. What is the difference between active wireless scanning and passive wireless scanning?

_____

_____

2. Describe the steps involved in performing a forensic investigation in a wireless environment.

_____

_____

3. What is a rogue access point?

_____

_____

4. How can an attacker hijack wireless network traffic?

_____

_____

5. How do electronic emanations help an attacker access a wireless network?

_____

_____

6. How is security provided for the connection between devices and wireless access points?

_____

_____

7. Describe what should be included in a report for a forensic investigation involving a wireless network.

_____

_____

8. What does an investigator need to do to determine if an access point is a rogue access point?

_____

_____

Hands-On Projects

1. Perform the following steps:
   - Navigate to Chapter 1 of the Student Resource Center.
   - Open Active Wireless Protection.pdf and read the content.
2. Perform the following steps:
   - Navigate to Chapter 1 of the Student Resource Center.
   - Open defending_wireless.pdf and read the content.
3. Perform the following steps:
   - Navigate to Chapter 1 of the Student Resource Center.
   - Open examining-wireless-access-points.pdf and read the content.
4. Perform the following steps:
   - Navigate to Chapter 1 of the Student Resource Center.
   - Open prevent wireless from attack.pdf and read the content.

Chapter 2

PDA Forensics

Objectives

After completing this chapter, you should be able to:

- Identify a personal digital assistant (PDA)
- Understand what information is stored in PDAs
- Recognize PDA components
- Understand PDA generic states
- Understand PDA security issues
- Take PDA forensic steps
- Use PDA forensic tools
- Implement countermeasures

Key Terms

Smartphone   a cellular phone with the features of a personal digital assistant

Introduction to PDA Forensics

A personal digital assistant, or PDA, is a small, lightweight handheld device. It can be used for communication, computation, and information storage and retrieval capabilities for both personal and business applications. It was originally designed as a personal organizer and has since developed into a versatile digital device.

Most PDAs include a small keyboard, although many newer devices instead have an electronic touch-sensitive liquid crystal pad that can receive handwriting as input.

PDAs can be synchronized with desktop and notebook computers for data exchange. Synchronization updates data on both systems to reflect the most recent additions and changes to their shared databases. This prevents data loss if the device is lost, stolen, or destroyed. PDAs are usually synchronized with the PC by using synchronization software bundled with the handheld, such as HotSync Manager with Palm OS handhelds and Microsoft ActiveSync with Windows Mobile handhelds.

Common PDA features include:

- Note taking
- Calculator
- Clock
- Calendar
- Address book
- Spreadsheets
- E-mail and Internet access
- Video and audio recording
- Built-in infrared, Bluetooth, and WiFi
- Radio and music players
- Games
- GPS (Global Positioning System)

Information Stored in PDAs

Because PDAs and cellular phones with PDA functionality (called *smartphones*) are used to store sensitive and confidential information, care should be taken to protect them. PDA devices store the following types of information:

- Business and personal notes
- Business and personal contacts
- Documents
- Passwords
- E-mails
- Bank records
- Company information
- Images and videos

PDA Characteristics

Most PDA devices have the following characteristics:

- Most PDA devices are made up of the following parts:
  - Microprocessor
  - Read-only memory (ROM)
  - Random-access memory (RAM)
  - Hardware keys and other user interfaces
  - Liquid crystal display, sometimes touch sensitive
- The operating system of the device is held in ROM.
- PDAs use different varieties of ROM, such as flash ROM that can be erased and programmed electronically.
- The operating system, application programs, and data currently in use are kept in volatile RAM so that they can be quickly reached by the processor. It needs a constant power supply to be active; failure or exhaustion of batteries results in information loss.
- Newer PDAs have system-level microprocessors that reduce the number of chips required and increase memory capacity.

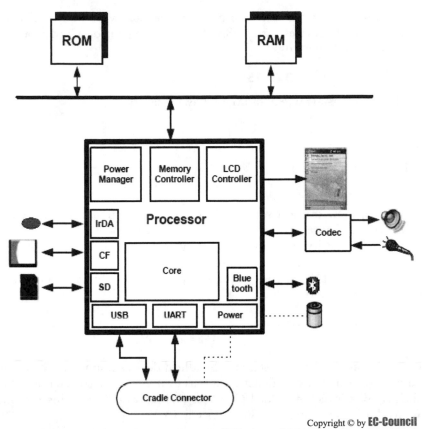

Figure 2-1   This diagram shows a modern PDA's hardware components.

- In addition to onboard memory, PDAs have memory-card readers, such as Secure Digital (SD) card slots.
- Many PDAs have built-in infrared, Bluetooth, and WiFi.

Figure 2-1 shows the relationship between the main components of a modern PDA.

Palm OS

Palm OS is an embedded operating system. Old Palm devices used 16- and 32-bit processors based on the Motorola DragonBall MC68328 family of microprocessors, while newer devices use ARM architecture-based StrongARM and XScale microprocessors.

In Palm OS PDA devices, the OS and certain applications are stored in ROM, while user data and other applications are stored in RAM. There are some add-on utilities available on the ROM used to back up Personal Information Management (PIM) data. This OS system software arranges both RAM and ROM on the same memory module, known as a card. A PDA device can contain any number of cards or none at all.

In Palm OS, the total available RAM is divided into two areas: dynamic RAM and storage RAM. Dynamic RAM is analogous to the RAM installed on desktop computers, and it is used as space for temporary allocation. The storage RAM acts like a hard drive on a desktop computer. Both types of RAM retain their contents when the device is off.

Memory in Palm OS is arranged in chunks known as records. These records are grouped into a database, which is a file in Palm File Format (PFF). These files are one of the following types:

- *Palm database*: Record database that stores user data such as contact lists and application data
- *Palm resource*: Contains application code and user interface objects
- *Palm query application*: World Wide Web contents

In Palm OS, all the applications share the same dynamic RAM so that they can use each other's data. Newer Palm OS devices use two expansion modes for more functionality, called Palm Universal Connector System and Palm Expansion Card Slot.

Palm Universal Connector System helps the device to interact with GPS receivers, wireless modems, keyboards, and other peripherals devices using USB. The Palm Expansion Card Slot accepts MultiMedia cards (MMCs) and Secure Digital (SD) cards.

Architecture of Palm OS Devices

The architecture of Palm OS is arranged into the following layers:

- Application
- Operating system
- Software API and hardware drivers
- Hardware

The software API helps execute software applications under different hardware environments. Developers can easily bypass the API and access the processor directly, giving more control over the processor. Sometimes, this accessibility increases security risks because of some malicious applications. Palm OS does not restrict access to the code and data, so anyone can access and modify it.

Palm OS provides some built-in security features. It provides the ability to lock the device when it is turned off, requiring a password to resume.

Windows CE

Microsoft has developed an operating system for handheld devices known as Windows CE. This OS supports multitasking and multithreaded environments, and has evolved and been renamed Pocket PC, then Windows Mobile. Nevertheless, Windows Embedded Compact (Windows CE) remains the underlying core operating system. Windows Mobile 6 is powered by Windows CE 5.2.

Windows CE runs on different processors, but mainly on devices having XScale, ARM, or SHx processors. The system's RAM stores the PIM and other user data, while the ROM stores the operating system and other supporting applications. The RAM in a Windows CE system is divided into two sections called the object store and the program memory. The object store serves as a permanent virtual RAM disk, and data is retained there by a backup power supply, even if the main power supply is interrupted. Windows CE supports one or more card slots such as CompactFlash (CF) or Secure Digital (SD). Most Pocket PC devices use lithium-ion batteries. The batteries should be charged often to prevent data loss.

Architecture of Windows CE

The architecture of Windows CE is arranged into the following layers:

- Application
- Operating system
- Original equipment manufacturer (OEM)
- Hardware

The original equipment manufacturer (OEM) layer is present in between the operating system layer and the hardware layer. The OEM layer contains the OEM adaptation layer (OAL), drivers, and configuration files. It handles functions such as system startup, interrupt handling, power management, profiling, timer, and clock. OAL allows OEM to operate Power PC on that specific platform.

In the operating system layer, the Windows CE kernel and device drivers are present. These device drivers help the kernel recognize the device and establish communication between software and hardware. Drivers are either monolithic or layered. Monolithic drivers apply their interfaces as an action directly on the device they control, while layered drivers divide this implementation into an upper layer and a lower layer. The upper layer exposes the driver's native or stream interface, while the lower layer interacts with the hardware.

The operating system also contains the graphics, windowing, and events subsystem (GWES). It provides the interface between the user, applications, and the OS. GWES integrates the graphics device interface (GDI), window manager, and event manager. It consists of two components: the user component, which handles messages, events, and input from keyboard and mouse; and the GDI, which draws the graphics, text, and images.

Objects in Windows CE are stored in three types of persistent storage: file system, registry, and property databases. The Windows CE system stores the files both in RAM and ROM. Files stored in RAM have the same name as those in ROM. The actual RAM file shadows the ROM file. Users who want to access the shadowed file can only gain access to the RAM version. When the user deletes the RAM file, the ROM file is accessible.

Property databases are repositories in which data can be stored, searched, and retrieved. The Windows CE registry stores all setting information related to applications, drivers, system configuration, and user data. This registry is stored in RAM.

Windows CE supports these four types of memory:

1. RAM
2. Expansion RAM
3. ROM
4. Persistent storage

Linux-Based PDAs

Linux provides a multitasking, multithreading 32-bit operating system for PDAs.

Architecture of the Linux OS for PDAs

Linux includes features such as:

- Memory management
- Process and thread creation
- Interprocess communication mechanisms
- Interrupt handling
- Execute-in-place (XIP) ROM file systems
- RAM file systems
- Flash management
- TCP/IP networking

The Linux kernel consists of modular components and subsystems that include device drivers, protocols, scheduler, memory manager, virtual file system, and resource allocator. The Linux kernel can be expanded using a programming interface. Processing starts from the system call interface making a request to the hardware. The hardware provides services to the kernel, and results coming from the kernel go to the system call interface.

Linux has security features such as user identification and authentication, access control, encryption techniques, Point-to-Point Tunneling Protocol (PPTP), Internet Protocol Security (IPSec), and Secure Shell (SSH). Even with these security features, Linux-based PDAs are vulnerable to authentication attacks.

PDA Generic States

Most computing devices such as desktop systems have only two states: on or off. Handheld devices such as PDAs, however, have different states, such as the following:

- *Nascent state*: The first state of the device when it is received from the manufacturer is the nascent state. In this state, devices do not have any user data, only factory configuration settings. The device returns to the nascent state after a hard reset or battery drain.
- *Active state*: In this state, devices are powered on and perform different tasks. Devices can be customized by the user and contain user data. Devices can be turned back to active state by performing a soft reset operation.
- *Quiescent state*: This is the sleep mode of the device, which conserves battery power to maintain the user's data and perform other background activities. The device can be returned back to quiescent state by pressing the power button in the active or semiactive state.
- *Semiactive state*: This state is partway between active and quiescent. The device usually is sent into this state by a timer. The timer is triggered when the device becomes inactive for some period, and the semiactive state allows battery life to be preserved by dimming the display and taking other appropriate actions. The semiactive state becomes active when a screen tap, button press, or soft reset occurs.

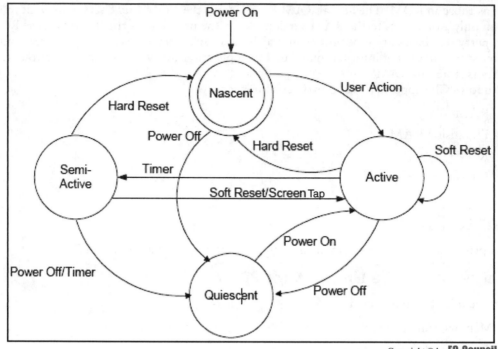

Figure 2-2   PDAs are always in one of four distinct states.

Devices not supporting the semiactive state go straight from the active state to the quiescent state after a certain period of inactivity. If the device is off, then it is considered to be in the quiescent state. Figure 2-2 shows the relationship of the four states.

PDA Security Issues

PDA security issues include:

- Password theft
- Virus attacks
- Data corruption
- Application vulnerabilities
- Data theft
- Wireless vulnerabilities
- Device theft

The major security issue with the PDA is the theft of the device itself. The best precaution to overcome this threat is by securing the data on the device in standalone mode (a mode in which the device is not connected to a wireless service provider).

Viruses can also pose a significant risk. There are also some vulnerabilities in programming languages such as Java and frameworks such as ActiveX, commonly used by PDA Web browsers.

PDAs that use wireless services or wireless ports are also vulnerable to wireless attacks. The best solution to protect PDAs from wireless attacks is to install a VPN client on the PDA and encrypt the connection.

Password theft can be reduced by using a lengthy secure password containing alphanumeric characters and symbols in order to make it more difficult to crack.

ActiveSync and HotSync Features

To protect mobile devices and data, it is necessary to understand the connectivity of devices with each other. Desktop synchronization with mobile devices is considered connectionless access.

ActiveSync synchronizes Windows-based PDAs and smartphones with desktop computers. An Active-Sync handheld is connected to a desktop PC via its cradle. The user can choose to protect ActiveSync with a password.

HotSync is the process of synchronizing elements between a Palm handheld device and a desktop PC. It will synchronize the user's Microsoft Outlook inbox, contact list, and calendar, as well as tasks and notes.

ActiveSync Attacks

ActiveSync allows an unlimited number of password attempts. An attacker can try to get the ActiveSync password though password sniffing or a brute force/dictionary attack.

When the user saves the password on the desktop computer, the attacker can easily access it after gaining access to the desktop. This allows the attacker to install malicious software on the PDA, such as a keylogger that will record all activity done with the PDA.

HotSync Attacks

Palm devices are vulnerable to HotSync attacks. While handling the HotSync feature, various viruses, Trojans, and other spyware can be transmitted. The Palm OS opens TCP ports 14237 and 14238 and also UDP port 14237 during the HotSync process. Attackers can open connections to these ports and access private information or send malicious code.

PDA Forensic Steps

Before starting an investigation, an investigator needs to consider the following questions:

- What kind of investigation needs to be done?
- How should the PDA be handled?
- Can critical data on the PDA remain secure during the examination?

Computer forensic investigators handling PDAs need a basic understanding of the features of various types of PDAs available on the market. The investigators must take care while examining the PDA because any wrong step would lead to the loss of valuable and case-related information. The following are the basic steps in PDA forensics:

1. Secure and evaluate the scene.
2. Seize the evidence.
3. Identify the evidence.
4. Preserve the evidence.
5. Acquire information.
6. Examine and analyze the information.
7. Document everything.
8. Make the report.

Points to Remember While Conducting an Investigation

An investigator must remember the following if the PDA device is switched on:

- Preserve the device in an active state with sufficient power. A suitable power adaptor must be connected to the device with the cable going through the evidence bag.
- A photograph of the device must be taken to show the current state of the device during collection.
- If the device charge is low, charge the battery with a suitable power adaptor.

An investigator must remember the following if the PDA device is switched off:

- Leave the device in the off state.
- Switch on the device to record the current battery state of the device.
- A photograph of the device must be taken to show the state of the device during collection.

An investigator must remember the following if the PDA device is in its cradle:

- Avoid all further communication activities.
- Remove the connection to the desktop computer to avoid any further communication.
- Seize the cradle and the cords connected to the PDA and place them in the evidence bag.

An investigator must remember the following if the PDA device is not in its cradle:

- Seize the cradle and the cords connected to the PDA and place them in the evidence bag.

An investigator must remember the following if wireless is on:

- Avoid all further communication activities.
- Take steps to eliminate any wireless activity by packing the device in an envelope, then in an antistatic bag, and finally in an isolation envelope.
- Remove any wireless-enabled cards and keep them separate.

An investigator must remember the following if a card is present in the expansion card slot:

- See to it that any further activity inside the device is not initiated.
- Do not remove any of the peripheral or media cards from their slots.

An investigator must remember the following if a card is not present in the expansion card slot:

- Immediately seize all related peripheral and media cards.

An investigator must remember the following if the expansion sleeve is removed from its place:

- Locate the expansion sleeve and preserve it in a separate container.
- Seize other associated peripherals and media cards.

Secure and Evaluate the Scene

An investigation is handled in different ways depending on the type of incident, the gravity of the incident, and the experience of the investigator. Digital evidence investigation is somewhat different from general crime investigation.

The first step in PDA crime investigation is to secure and evaluate the scene. The following are some of the points that the investigator must follow while evaluating the scene:

- Restrict the entry of unauthorized persons at the scene.
- Secure all devices at the scene, including digital devices such as PDAs and laptops.
- Maintain the integrity of both traditional and electronic evidence.
- Take digital photographs of the scene and the evidence. Photographs should be taken from each side of the evidence.
- Document the scene, including the exact location and time.
- Document the condition of each device at the scene, including power status (on or off).
- Maintain the chain of custody with documents and photographs.
- Interview every person who was present at the scene.
- Evaluate the scene and prepare a search plan for the next investigation.

Seize the Evidence

After documenting and photographing the scene and evidence, the investigator must collect the evidence. He or she should seize handheld and computer devices such as PDA devices, cradles, power supplies, associated peripherals, media, and accessories. The investigator should also collect memory devices such as SD, MMC, or CF cards; microdrives; and USB flash drives. He or she should also collect nonelectronic evidence such as written passwords, handwritten notes, and computer printouts.

While collecting the devices, the investigator should take the following precautions:

- The evidence should not be damaged.
- Use proper gloves to collect the evidence.

- Collect and keep the evidence in bags.
- Keep the evidence away from any unauthorized persons.
- Keep the evidence in a secure place.
- Maintain the proper chain of custody.

Identify the Evidence

The forensic examiner's first duty is to identify the type of device being investigated. The suspect can modify the PDA device before the investigation by changing the logos on the PDA, modifying the operating system, completely replacing the operating system, or making the operating system appear and behave differently than before. If PDAs are turned on, the type of device can be identified by the operating system, which is more accurate than simply looking at a logo.

Though Pocket PC and Palm OS are the two dominant operating systems used in PDAs, which are manufactured to run one OS, they have the capability to run other operating systems. Each OS has particular applications within the main GUI, such as Word, Explorer, Memo Pad, and Terminal. Other clues that help to identify the devices are the cradle's interface, the manufacturer's serial number, the cradle type, and the power supply.

Preserve the Evidence

The following are some precautions to be taken while preserving the evidence:

- Keep the evidence in a secure place.
- The PDA should not be switched on if already off.
- If the PDA has only a single rechargeable battery, connect the power adaptor to it with the cable passing through the evidence bag.
- If the PDA is found switched on, keep it in active mode until a forensic investigator examines it.
- Pack the PDA in an envelope and seal it to restrict physical access.
- Keep the evidence away from extreme temperature and high humidity.
- Keep the evidence away from magnetic sources.
- Keep the evidence away from moisture, dust, physical shock, and static electricity.
- Keep the evidence away from shock and excessive vibrations.
- Give proper labels to evidence containers.
- Do not fold, bend, or scratch computer media such as discs and removable media.
- Maintain the proper chain of custody.

Acquire the Information

Acquisition means obtaining the data from digital devices, peripheral devices, and media. Data acquisition at the scene avoids data loss due to battery depletion and damage. However, it can be difficult or even impossible to collect data at the scene rather than at the laboratory.

Before acquiring data from the device, the investigator has to identify the device. Once that is accomplished, it is best to make an image of the device memory. An image is a bit-for-bit copy of the original that is created to protect the original from alteration. This image can be created with the help of forensic tools like EnCase.

Before acquiring the data, the investigator must create a connection between the forensic workstation and the device. The data-acquisition tools and their versions must be documented. The investigator should acquire the information with multiple different tools such as PDA Seizure and Palm dd to be certain of the results.

After acquiring the data, the investigator must confirm that the entire contents of the device were captured correctly, by comparing the RAM/ROM's size.

Data-Acquisition Techniques

In addition to data-acquisition tools, the following are some other techniques used for data acquisition:

- Find out different vulnerabilities in the device or system and try to exploit them. Most devices have weak authentication mechanisms and are vulnerable to misconfigured network services and protocols, opening them to buffer overflow attacks. Try to discover the vulnerabilities in other features such as serial, USB, IrDA, Bluetooth, WiFi, and GSM/GPRS facilities. If successful exploitation occurs, all information from the device can be obtained.

- If the device is protected by a password, apply brute force techniques to access the password. Employ password-cracking tools such as Hydra or Cain and Abel.
- Access the device's information using backdoors supplied by the manufacturer.
- Extract data from memory chips independently of the device.
- Data also can be extracted by using reverse-engineering techniques. Reverse engineering includes retrieving the operating system code from the ROM of another PDA device with the same specifications and discovering the vulnerabilities in that code.

Examine and Analyze the Information

The examiner and analyzer may be the same person or different people. Both must have knowledge of data acquisition and examination tools, which help determine the content and state of the data. Information stores may be hidden or obscured. An analyst tries to separate the relevant information from the irrelevant information. The following should be performed while examining and analyzing information:

- Analyze the evidence in the device, such as:
  - Address books
  - Documents
  - E-mail
  - Passwords
  - Appointments and calendar information
  - Phonebooks
  - Text and voice messages
  - Images and videos
- Review any logs present and the date/time stamps in the file system.
- Check the creation and modification times of the files.
- Find out the author of files.
- Create a timeline of events.
- Recover hidden information.
- Use steganalysis tools such as Stegdetect to extract hidden information.
- Use cryptanalysis tools such as Crank and Jipher to reveal encrypted information.
- Use password-cracking tools such as Cain and Abel and Hydra if the information is password protected.
- Use various video players to open video files.
- Check the last dialed number or coordinates to destinations.
- Find out the tools used.
- From the analysis, try to discover:
  - What exactly happened
  - When the event occurred
  - Who was involved
  - How the event occurred

Document Everything

The forensic examiner must take care that each and every step during the investigation is documented and the findings are recorded. A chain of evidence must be maintained in order to prove the integrity of the evidence in court. The evidence gathered must be precisely accounted for and identified. The documentation process also includes the labeling process.

While labeling the seized PDA during investigation, the forensic examiner must record the case number, a brief description about the case, his or her signature, and the date and time of the evidence collection. The scene must also be photographed and recorded along with a report documenting the state of the PDA device during seizure and examination. All visible information on the seized PDA device must be documented. Any digital device connected to the PDA must be photographed with all the peripherals, cables, cradles, power connectors, removable media, and other connections. These photographs must also be documented along with the report.

The state of the contents of the PDA screen must be photographed if the device is in an active or semiactive state, and these contents must be recorded manually. Other features of the PDA, such as a blinking activity indicator or physical connectivity, should also be recorded. The forensic examiner must also view and document any volatile data that is not displayed and could affect other evidence. The chain of custody is a simple method of documenting the complete handling and passage of evidence throughout the life of the case.

Make the Report

The final report should be a detailed summary of the steps taken to investigate the crime and the result of the investigation. Reporting depends on each participant involved in the investigation, as well as their actions, observations, and test results. A good report contains full documentation about the evidence, notes, photographs, and tools used in the investigation.

A forensic investigator should follow the predefined template for creating the investigative report. This report should include the case and its source, outline the test results and findings, and bear the signature of the individual responsible for its contents. In general, the report should include the following:

- Identity of the reporting agency
- Case identifier or submission number
- Case investigator
- Identity of the submitter
- Date of receipt
- Date of report
- List of items submitted for examination, with their serial numbers and model numbers
- Identity and signature of the examiner
- The equipment and setup used in the examination
- A brief explanation about the investigating steps such as string searches, graphic image searches, and deleted file recovery
- Other supporting materials such as documents about the evidence, printouts of particular items of evidence, and digital copies of evidence
- Details of findings:
  - Specific files related to the request
  - Other files, such as deleted files, that support the findings
  - String searches, keyword searches, and text string searches
  - Internet-related evidences including Web site traffic analysis, chat logs, cache files, e-mail, and newsgroup activity
  - Graphic image analysis
  - Data analysis
  - Description of the relevant programs used for examination
  - Data hiding techniques such as encryption and steganography
  - Data extracted from hidden attributes, hidden partitions, and file name anomalies
- Conclusions

Tool: PDASecure

PDASecure provides security to a PDA's data from theft, loss, or corruption. It includes Trusted Mobility server software that allows the administrator to control the use of handheld devices on his or her network. When a

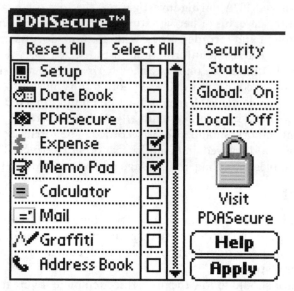

Figure 2-3 PDASecure protects the data on PDA devices.

PDA uses Pocket PC, PDA Secure allows the administrator to set a time and date range to monitor login attempts, infrared transmission, and the use of applications.

PDASecure provides enhanced password protection, as well as encryption, device locking, and permanent deletion of selected data. The program's PDA interface is shown in Figure 2-3.

Tool: Device Seizure

Device Seizure examines cell phone and PDA data. It is capable of command-line acquisition, deleted data recovery, full data dumps of certain cell phone models, logical and physical acquisitions of PDAs, data cable access, and advanced reporting. Device Seizure's Windows interface is shown in Figure 2-4.

Device Seizure can acquire the following data:

- SMS history (text messages)
- Deleted SMS (text messages)
- Phonebook (both stored in the memory of the phone and on the SIM card)
- Call history
  - Received calls
  - Dialed numbers
  - Missed calls
  - Call dates and durations
- Datebook
- Scheduler
- Calendar
- To-do list
- Filesystem (physical memory dumps)
  - System files
  - Multimedia files
  - Java files
  - Deleted data
  - Quicknotes

Figure 2-4 Device Seizure examines cell phone and PDA data.

- GPS waypoints, tracks, routes, etc.
- RAM/ROM
- PDA databases
- E-mail
- Registry (Windows Mobile devices)

Tool: DS Lite

Paraben's DS Lite is a Device Seizure and CSI Stick file-viewing and analysis tool. CSI Stick is a portable cell phone forensic and data gathering tool that looks like a USB thumb drive. DS Lite can open Device Seizure files (.pds) and data acquired from CSI Stick for advanced analysis, file viewing, searching, and reporting. This allows any case agent or investigator to view and analyze data acquired by either CSI Stick or Device Seizure. DS Lite is pictured in Figure 2-5.

Its features include the following:

- Reads CSI Stick and Device Seizure acquisition files
- Comprehensive analysis of text messages, address books, call logs, and more
- Verification of file integrity with use of MD5 and SHA1 hash values
- Built-in file viewing of proprietary files
- Built-in searching and bookmarking
- Text and hex viewing options available for data
- Analyzes PDA data files stored on PCs
- Windows CE registry viewer
- Image viewing for graphic information, including data carving for multimedia files for most devices
- Comprehensive HTML and text reporting
- Text searching (including Unicode) and hex information in the acquired data
- Exports acquired data to PC
- Viewing acquired data with external viewer

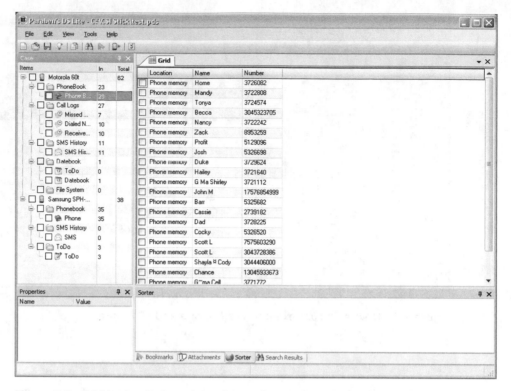

Figure 2-5 DS Lite is a lightweight viewer for Device Seizure output files.

Tool: EnCase

EnCase is used for acquiring and imaging the evidence. It allows the recovery of deleted files and provides hash generation of individual files, data capture, and documentation. EnCase allows the creation of a physical bit-stream image of the source device that helps the investigator to search and examine the contents of the device without affecting the integrity of the original data.

EnCase has a bookmarking feature that saves bookmarks in case files. The case files can then be exchanged for collaboration. EnCase is shown in Figure 2-6.

Tool: SIM Card Seizure

SIM Card Seizure recovers deleted SMS/text messages and performs comprehensive analysis of SIM card data. It takes the SIM card acquisition and analysis components from Paraben's Device Seizure and puts them into a specialized SIM card forensic acquisition and analysis tool. SIM Card Seizure includes both software and a SIM card reader. The following are some of the features of SIM Card Seizure:

- Calculates MD5 and SHA1 hash values
- Provides a search function
- Recovers deleted SMS data
- Provides bookmarking options
- Includes a report creation wizard

SIM Card Seizure can extract the following data:

- Phase ID
- SST: SIM service table
- ICCID: Serial number
- LP: Preferred languages variable

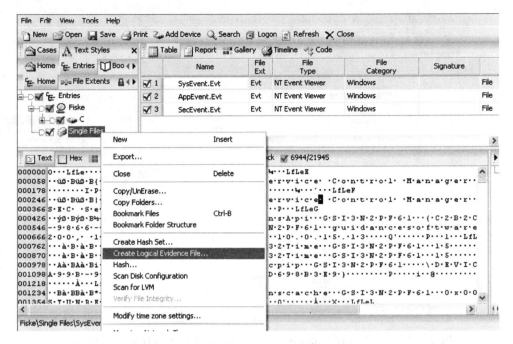

Figure 2-6 EnCase encapsulates bookmarks so they can be shared.

- SPN: Service provider name
- MSISDN: Subscriber phone number
- AND: Short dial number
- FDN: Fixed numbers
- LND: Last dialed numbers
- EXT1: Dialing extension
- EXT2: Dialing extension
- GID1: Groups
- GID2: Groups
- SMS: Text messages
- SMSP: Text message parameters
- SMSS: Text message status
- CBMI: Preferred network messages
- PUCT: Charges per unit
- ACM: Charge counter
- ACMmax: Charge limit
- HPLMNSP: HPLMN search period
- PLMNsel: PLMN selector
- FPLMN: Forbidden PLMNs
- CCP: Capability configuration parameter
- ACC: Access control class
- IMSI: International mobile subscriber identity

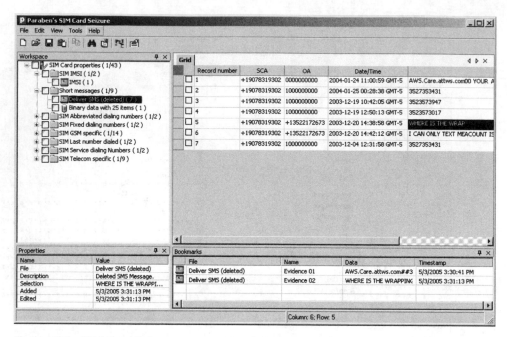

Figure 2-7 SIM Card Seizure can extract data from a cell phone's SIM card.

- LOCI: Location information
- BCCH: Broadcast control channels
- KC: Ciphering key

SIM Card Seizure is pictured in Figure 2-7.

Tool: Palm dd (pdd)

Palm dd, or pdd, is a free Windows-based tool for Palm OS memory imaging and forensic acquisition. The Palm OS Console Mode is used to acquire memory card information and to create a bit-for-bit image of the selected memory region. No data is modified on the target device, and the user of the PDA cannot detect the data retrieval.

The data retrieved by pdd includes all user applications and databases. pdd is a command-line-driven application without features such as graphics libraries, report generation, search facilities, and bookmarking capabilities. Once the information has been acquired, two files are generated: one that contains device-specific information (e.g., OS version, processor type, and sizes of RAM and ROM), and another that contains a bit-by-bit image of the device. All output is in binary form, some of which happens to be ASCII characters. Files created from pdd can be imported into a forensic tool, such as EnCase, to aid analysis; otherwise, the default tool is a hex editor. pdd does not provide hash values for the information acquired. However, a separate procedure can be used to obtain needed hash values.

pdd is pictured in Figure 2-8.

Tool: Duplicate Disk

The Duplicate Disk (dd) utility is similar to pdd. It executes directly on the PDA and creates a bit-by-bit image of the device on an external storage device. Caution should be exercised, since dd may destroy parts of the file system if used incorrectly. As with pdd, dd produces binary data output, some of which contains ASCII character information. Images created with dd may be imported for examination into a forensic tool, such as EnCase, if the file system is supported. A dd-created image may also be mounted in loopback mode on a file-system-compatible Linux machine for analysis. The standard version of dd does not provide hash values for the information acquired. However, a separate procedure can be used to obtain needed hash values.

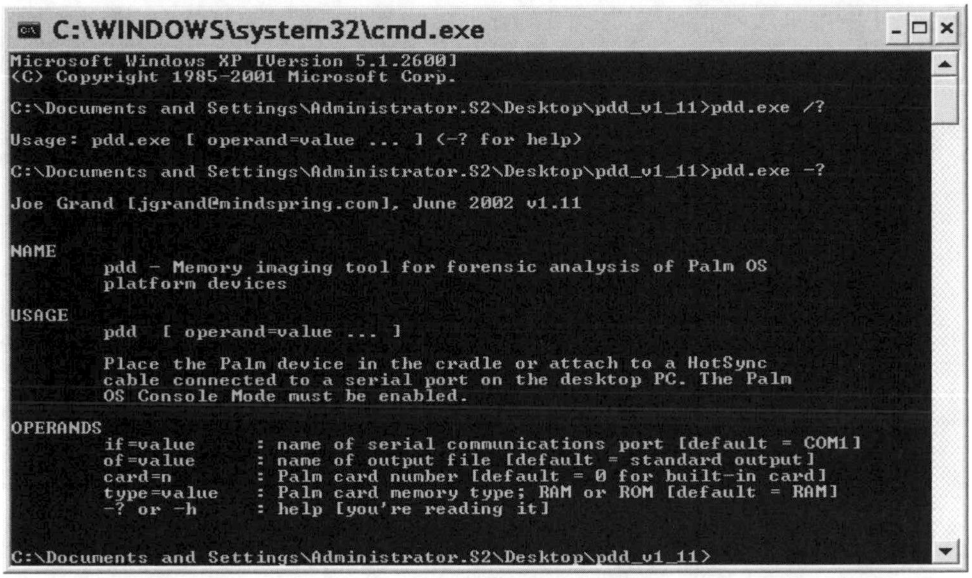

Figure 2-8   pdd is a command-line tool for creating images of Palm OS memory.

Tool: Forensic Software - Pocket PC

Forensic Software - Pocket PC extracts files, database records, operating system registry records, and phone information from Pocket PCs. It shows contacts, model information, IMEI number, SIM information, and manufacturer details. It can also show the OS type and version, processor architecture, memory usage, and other related information. The program is shown in Figure 2-9.

Tool: Mobile Phone Inspector

Mobile Phone Inspector provides detailed information of mobile phone memory and SIM memory status, including mobile manufacturer name, mobile model number, mobile IMEI number, SIM IMSI number, signal quality, and battery status of any supported mobile phone. It also provides details on the phone's saved contact list. Mobile Phone Inspector is shown in Figure 2-10.

Tool: Recovery Memory Card

Recovery Memory Card recovers and restores files and folders from memory card storage media, even if the media is corrupted. It supports many memory card formats, including the following:

- PC Card
- CompactFlash (I, II)
- SmartMedia
- MultiMedia card (MMC)
- Secure Digital card
- Mini-SD card
- Micro-SD card
- xD-picture card

Recovery Memory Card is pictured in Figure 2-11.

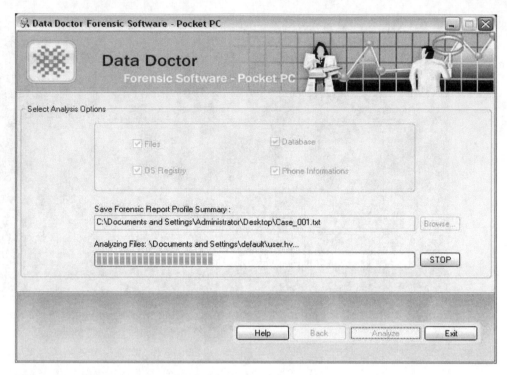

Figure 2-9 Forensic Software - Pocket PC extracts information from Pocket PC devices.

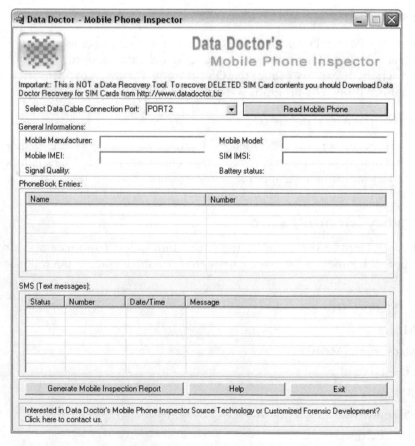

Figure 2-10 Mobile Phone Inspector extracts data from mobile phone memory and SIM cards.

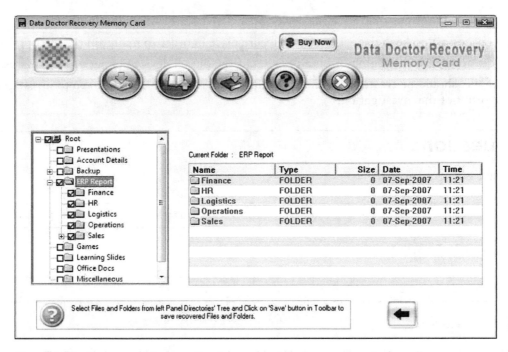

Figure 2-11 Recovery Memory Card recovers data from corrupted media.

PDA Security Countermeasures

As mobile phones and PDAs are becoming more technologically advanced, attackers are finding different ways to target victims. The following are a few good defenses:

- Install a firewall.
- Disable all HotSync and ActiveSync features not in use.
- Use a strong password.
- Do not store passwords on a desktop PC.
- Install antivirus software on the device.
- Encrypt any critical data on the device.
- Do not use untrusted or insecure Wi-Fi access points.

Chapter Summary

- A personal digital assistant (PDA) is a handheld device. It has communication, computation, and information storage and retrieval capabilities for personal and business use.
- While PDAs and smartphones can greatly enhance an employee's productivity, the amount of sensitive and confidential information stored in PDAs increases the risk of information theft.
- PDAs have different hardware features and capabilities depending upon their operating systems.
- Microsoft has developed the operating system for handheld devices known as Pocket PC.
- A PDA has four generic states: nascent state, active state, quiescent state, and semiactive state.
- ActiveSync synchronizes Windows-based PDAs and smartphones with desktop computers.
- Computer forensic investigators handling a PDA need a basic understanding of the features of the various types of PDAs available.

- The investigator must preserve the device in an active state with sufficient power.
- It is necessary to keep the evidence at a secure place in order to maintain the integrity of the evidence.
- Acquisition means imaging or obtaining data from digital device, its peripheral devices, and media.
- A report should be created including a detailed summary of the steps taken to investigate the crime and the result of the investigation.

Review Questions

1. What is a smartphone?

   _____

   _____

2. What is ActiveSync?

   _____

   _____

3. What is HotSync?

   _____

   _____

4. Name five common PDA features.

   _____

   _____

5. Name five pieces of information stored in PDAs.

   _____

   _____

6. Describe the four generic PDA states.

   _____

   _____

7. Describe the steps involved in PDA forensic investigations.

   _____

   _____

8. Describe four data-acquisition techniques an investigator can use with PDAs.

   _____

   _____

   _____

Hands-On Projects

1. Perform the following steps:
   - Connect a PDA to the PC.
   - Navigate to Chapter 2 of the Student Resource Center.
   - Install and launch the PDA Seizure program.
   - Click the **Acquire** icon in the toolbar.

2. Perform the following steps:

- Navigate to Chapter 2 of the Student Resource Center.
- Read the following documents:
  - pda_forensics1104.pdf
  - PDAForensics.pdf
  - PDA Forensic analysis.pdf

iPod and iPhone Forensics

Objectives

After completing this chapter, you should be able to:

- Understand the iPod and the iPhone
- Perform iPod and iPhone forensics
- Retrieve evidence stored on iPods and iPhones
- Jailbreak the iPod Touch and iPhone
- Utilize tools for iPod and iPhone forensics

Key Terms

Jailbreaking   the process of unlocking the iPhone and iPod Touch to permit the installation of third-party applications

Introduction to iPod and iPhone Forensics

Apple's iPod, and its newer variant the iPhone, have quickly become the standard for digital media players and smartphones. In this chapter, you will learn how the iPod and iPhone can be used to store data, and how you can retrieve that data.

iPod and iPhone

The iPod is a portable media player designed by Apple Computer. It offers a large storage capacity, which can be used to store audio, video, and other data in various formats. MP3, M4A/AAC, protected AAC, AIFF, WAV, Audible audio book, and Apple Lossless audio file formats can be played on iPods. The classic iPods use hard drives to store data; the newer versions, such as the iPod Nano, iPod Shuffle, and iPod Touch, use flash memory. Music and video files are organized on the iPod using the iTunes software on a PC or Mac.

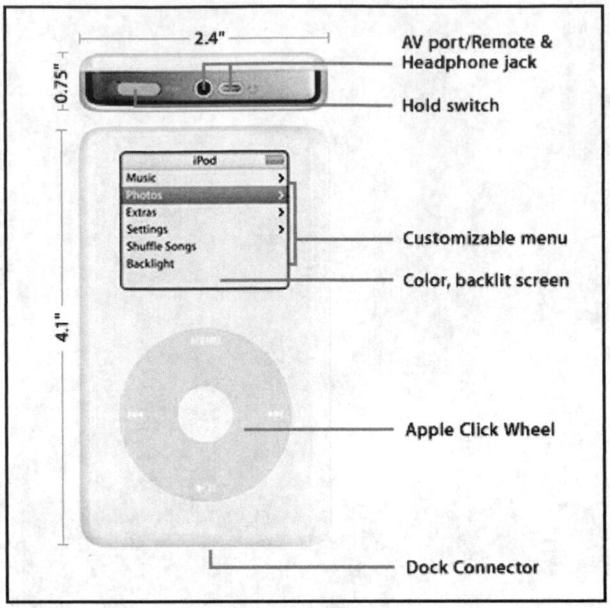

Figure 3-1 The standard iPod features a click wheel and a backlit screen.

The iPod Touch is an iPod with Wi-Fi and a multitouch interface, featuring the Safari Web browser and wireless access to the iTunes Store and YouTube. It uses the iPhone OS as its operating system.

Figure 3-1 shows the components of a standard iPod.

iPhone

The iPhone is an Internet-connected multimedia device with a multitouch screen. Most user interaction is handled through the touch screen, including a virtual keyboard for text entry. The iPhone includes the following standard features:

- Phone
- E-mail
- Safari Web browser
- Media player
- SMS text messaging
- Maps with GPS
- iTunes Store
- App Store
- Calendar
- YouTube
- Camera
- Stocks, weather, and notes
- Scientific calculator

What a Criminal Can Do with an iPod

The iPod's large storage capacity, small size, and rapid data transfer make it potentially useful for attackers in information theft. The iPod's popularity and image as an "innocent" media player has made it popular among criminals. Police have established connections between iPods and various crimes, and have successfully traced criminals using iPod investigations.

iPods can be hacked or customized using various techniques. They can be configured to work as external hard drives or to execute custom scripts. Criminals use iPods in a variety of ways, such as the following:

- To spread viruses and Trojans
- To store and distribute illegal images and videos
- To keep records of crimes, such as date and time
- To distribute contact information of other criminals

What a Criminal Can Do with an iPhone

In addition to all of the features of a standard iPod, the iPhone includes Internet connectivity and all of the features of a standard cell phone. This means that a criminal can use it for many additional activities, including the following:

- To steal user data, such as contact numbers, e-mail addresses, and SMS messages
- To connect the iPhone to another system to steal its data
- To send threatening or offensive SMS and MMS messages
- To manipulate SIM properties
- To clone SIM data
- To remove the service provider lock (SP-Lock) in order to free the iPhone from its network
- To send spam messages

iPhone OS Overview

The iPhone OS runs on both the iPhone and the iPod Touch. It is derived from Mac OS X, uses the Darwin foundation, and uses less than 300 MB of the device's total memory storage.

The iPhone OS has the following four abstraction layers:

1. The core OS layer provides the kernel environment, drivers, and basic interfaces of the operating system.
2. The core services layer provides the fundamental services for applications such as Address Book, Core Location, CFNetwork, Security, and SQLite.
3. The media layer provides graphics and media technologies such as Core Audio, OpenAL, and video technologies.
4. The Cocoa Touch layer consists of UI Kit and Foundation frameworks, which provide the user with tools for implementing graphical and event-driven applications.

iPhone Disk Partitions

The iPhone utilizes disk partitions in order to manage the information stored. It has a solid state NAND flash memory and is configured with the following two partitions by default:

1. The root partition is 300 MB, consisting of the operating system and all preloaded applications. By default, it is mounted as a read-only partition and stays in its original factory state for the life of the iPhone.
2. The user partition is all of the remaining space. It contains all of the user's data. It is mounted as /private/var on the iPhone.

Apple HFS+ and FAT32

iPods formatted with Mac computers use Apple's HFS+ file system, while those formatted on Windows use the FAT32 file system. When conducting forensic analysis of the iPod, investigators need to know with which type of system the iPod has been synchronized.

Application Formats

iPods use different file formats for storing different kinds of data. They use the standard vCard file format for storing contact information. This format exchanges electronic business cards. vCards contain personal information such as name and address, and they can be easily attached to e-mails.

Calendar entries are stored in the industry-standard vCalendar format, also known as the Personal Calendaring and Scheduling Exchange Format. Operating like vCard files, these can be used to exchange calendar and scheduling information.

Music can be stored in several different file formats. iPods can play MP3s, M4A/AACs, protected AACs, AIFFs, WAVs, and Apple Lossless audio file formats. Newer iPods can also play .m4v (H.264) and .mp4 (MPEG-4) video file formats, as well as unprotected WMA files from Windows machines. iPods use ID3 tags to sort audio files. ID3 tags are metadata containers used to store information such as the title, artist, album, and track number.

Users can store files on the device securely as encrypted or hidden files. They can also be used as a voice recorder or for photo storage by using third-party applications and accessories.

iPod and iPhone Forensics

iPod and iPhone forensics includes recovery and analysis of data and helps in tracing and prosecuting criminals in cases where iPods or iPhones were used in connection to a crime. It can also help in other criminal cases to obtain contact details and communication logs.

Evidence Stored on iPods and iPhones

iPods and iPhones can contain the following forensically relevant information:

- Text messages
- Calendar events
- Photos and videos
- Caches
- Logs of recent activity
- Map and satellite imagery
- Personal alarms
- Notes
- Music
- E-mail
- Web browsing activity
- Passwords and personal credentials
- Fragments of typed communication
- Voicemails
- Call history
- Contacts
- Information pertaining to interoperability with other devices
- Items of personal interest

Forensic Prerequisites

To correctly perform iPod forensics and get exact results, it is necessary to use the proper hardware and software investigation devices. The following are the necessary hardware devices required for iPod forensics:

- The iPod collected at the scene
- A Windows computer, where most of the investigation will take place, with the following minimum specifications:
  - Processor: AMD Athlon 64 2800
  - RAM: 512 MB
  - Hard drive: 160 GB

- A Macintosh computer with the following minimum specifications:
  - Processor: 500 MHz
  - RAM: 128 MB
  - Hard drive: 8 GB

In addition, the following software will be necessary:

- The newest Windows or Mac operating systems
- Data recovery tools such as Recover My iPod and iPod Data Recovery
- Forensic tools such as EnCase and Forensic Toolkit

Collecting iPods and iPhones Connected with Mac

An investigator should collect the iPod immediately if it is not connected to a computer. If the iPod is connected to a computer, the investigator should check whether the device is mounted. This can be determined by checking the iPod screen for a "Do Not Disconnect" sign. If that sign is not present, the device is not mounted and can be removed.

If it is mounted, the investigator needs to unmount the device before disconnecting it from the computer. To unmount the device, he or she must drag the **iPod** icon on the Macintosh desktop shown in Figure 3-2 to the **Trash**. While unmounting the device, the investigator must make sure to not disconnect it or unplug the computer.

Collecting iPods and iPhones Connected with Windows

In order to unmount an iPod from a Windows system, an investigator needs to right-click the **Safely Remove Hardware** icon in the System Tray and then click **Safely Remove Hardware**, as shown in Figure 3-3.

Disable Automatic Syncing

Automatic syncing is the synchronizing of information on the device with the information stored on the system. Disabling this prevents cross-contamination of iPod and iPhone data. The following are the steps to disable automatic syncing:

1. Open iTunes on the desktop machine.
2. Select **Preferences** from the iTunes menu.
3. Click the **Syncing** tab.
4. Check **Disable automatic syncing for all iPhones and iPods**.

Figure 3-2   Drag the **iPod** icon to the **Trash** to unmount it.

Figure 3-3   Always use **Safely Remove Hardware** to remove iPods from Windows machines.

Write Blocking

Write blocking prevents data alteration and maintains the integrity of data storage devices. Generally, in order to prevent the original evidence from being altered, imaging techniques are used. Imaging can be performed using software and hardware tools. Still, this image may sometimes get altered and produce different results.

Write blocking protects the evidence from any type of change and gives read-only access to the evidence. Hardware blockers are more reliable than software blockers, but they are more difficult to implement. Generally, hardware blockers are used for hard disks, but because of the greater cost of USB write-blocking hardware, many investigators prefer software blocking. Windows users can use software write blockers such as PDBLOCK and hardware write blockers such as WiebeTech Forensic SATADock. For Linux and Macintosh, there are commands available to perform write blocking.

Write Blocking in Different Operating Systems

Depending on the OS, there are different write-blocking techniques. In some operating systems, tools can be used to give read-only access, while in others, commands can be used. Generally, software write-blocking tools are used in Windows, while commands are used on Linux and Macintosh systems.

In Windows XP SP2 and above, an investigator can locate the following registry key:

HKEY_LOCAL_MACHINE\System\CurrentControlset\Control\StorageDevicePolicies

He or she can change this key value to the hex value of 0x00000001 and restart the computer. This change blocks write access to any USB storage devices. To reenable write access, the investigator can change this key value to 0x00000000 and restart the computer. This can also be achieved by using NCFS USB Write Blocker.

There are two techniques available in Linux to perform write blocking. The first is to modify the available source code of Linux itself to prevent writing to USB devices and then recompile. The second option is to modify the system configuration to prevent Linux from automatically mounting the iPod as a drive. This allows the investigator to use that device as a blocked device, and will allow the file system to be mounted as read only. In Ubuntu Live CD, automounting can be disabled by selecting **System**, then **Preferences**, and finally **Removable Drives and Media**. In the next window, uncheck all boxes and click **OK**.

Because Macintosh is mostly based on the concepts of Linux, write blocking the evidence using configuration methods is conceptually the same. These methods include the following:

- Preventing Mac OS from automatically mounting removable media
- Preventing iTunes from loading when iPod is connected
- Mounting the iPods with read-only access

Image the Evidence

Before acquiring the data from the original device, the investigator usually creates an image of the evidence. Imaging is the process of creating an exact bit-for-bit copy of the contents of a digital device. The main aim of imaging is to protect the original device from any alteration. There are several different data imaging tools available for the iPod, such as EnCase.

When an iPod is connected using its USB interface, it automatically switches to Disk Mode and gives the system direct access to the drive, which can make imaging inaccurate. Disk Mode can be stopped by toggling the **Hold** switch on and off. To force Disk Mode, an investigator can press the **Select** and **Menu** buttons until the Apple logo appears, and then immediately release the **Menu** and **Select** buttons and hold down the **Select** and **Play** buttons until the Disk Mode screen appears.

Because Disk Mode can cause inaccuracies, it is better to use imaging tools such as EnCase and GNU dd. Using hashing techniques such as MD5 ensures that the image and the original copy are the same. An investigator can use data recovery tools such as Recover My iPod and iPod Data Recovery to recover the data from these images.

View the iPod System Partition

The system partition of the iPod does not store the user's identifiable data. It includes factory default data such as the following:

- iPod OS
- Images used in the operation of the device
- Games and other default applications stored on the device

Because the formatting of this partition is unknown, the analyst should open this partition in a hex editor for analysis.

View the Data Partition

Depending on the type of iPod, it has a two or three partition structure. All iPods have both a system partition and a data partition. Windows iPods have just these two partitions, while Macintosh iPods have three. The extra partition in the Macintosh version is necessary due to the HFS+ file system. This third partition is split into a resource fork, with data partition file information, and a data fork containing the actual files.

The data partition on the iPod contains the user's unique information, including the following:

- Calendar entries
- Contact entries
- Note entries
- Hidden iPod_Control directory
- iTunes configuration information
- Stored media

This partition can be viewed by using Forensic Toolkit, EnCase, a hex editor, and various Linux and Macintosh analysis commands. This data partition has the same structure for both Windows and Macintosh iPods, and consists of the same files and directories.

Break Passcode to Access a Locked iPhone

If an iPhone is locked, an investigator can follow these steps to unlock it:

1. From the keypad, press the **Emergency Call** button.
2. Type *#301# followed by the green phone button.
3. Delete the previous entry by hitting the Delete key six times.
4. Type the number 0 followed by the green phone button.
5. Answer the call by pressing the green phone button.
6. End the call by pressing the red phone button.
7. Press the **Decline** button.
8. In the **Contacts** tab, press the + button at the top to create a new contact.
9. In the **Add new URL** tab, type **prefs:** and press the **Save** button.
10. Touch the **No Name** contact entry.
11. Click the **home page prefs:** button.
12. Click the **General** tab in the **Settings** menu.
13. Click the **Passcode Lock** tab.
14. Click the **Turn Passcode Off** button.
15. Return to the **General** tab by clicking the **Cancel** button.
16. Click **Auto-Lock** and reset it to **Never**.

Acquire DeviceInfo File

The \iPod_Control\iTunes\DeviceInfo file in the iPod contains several key pieces of information related to both the iPod and the computer used to set it up. This file is created by iTunes during the iPod's initial setup, which can only be performed while connected to a computer. The file contains the following information:

- Name given to the iPod
- Username logged into the computer
- Name of the computer

Figure 3-4   An iPod's DeviceInfo file is tied to the computer on which it was set up.

This only occurs if the iPod is set up using iTunes. The device information as viewed on the iPod itself is shown in Figure 3-4.

Acquire SysInfo File

The \iPod_Control\Device\SysInfo file is created by the iPod Updater software. This file is generated when the iPod is disconnected from the computer and connected to a power adapter. This file will not change after the device has been disconnected from the computer, and this time is considered the last restored time of the iPod.

This file contains the following information:

- Model number of the iPod (ModelNumStr)
- Serial number of the iPod (pszSerialNumber)
- Serial number the iPod presents to the computer (FireWireGUID)
- The FireWireGUID identifier identifies the connection of the iPod to a Windows computer (\Windows\setupapi.log), while the ModelNumStr identifies which iPod is connected to the computer

This file exists at the same location in both Windows and Mac OS. It also exists in both Windows and Mac OS formatted iPods at the same byte offset from the beginning of the drive, beginning at hexadecimal byte offset 0x5F02200. While using a hex editor, an investigator can search for hexadecimal byte offset 0x5F02200 or search for BoardHWName. If this doesn't work, the investigator can try searching for the serial number of the iPod, visible on the back cover of the iPod.

Recover IPSW File

IPSW is the iPod Touch and iPhone software update file format. The file contains the data for software restores and minor software updates. It also contains information on running, installed, and uninstalled applications. It is stored in the Library/iTunes/iPhone Software Updates directory on the iPhone. An IPSW file viewed using Mac OS can be seen in Figure 3-5.

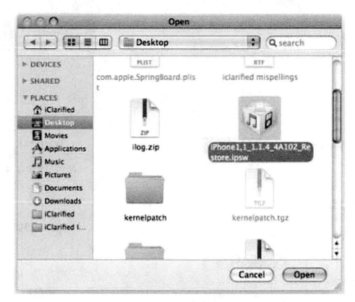

Figure 3-5   IPSW files contain software update data.

Figure 3-6   Connect an iPod to iTunes to view the firmware version.

Check the Internet Connection Status

An investigator can check the status of the device's Internet connection by looking for the following:

- An E icon shows connection to an EDGE network.
- A 3G icon shows connection to a third-generation network.
- Radiating signal bars show Wi-Fi connectivity.

View Firmware Version

To view the firmware version on an iPod, an investigator must first connect the device to iTunes. He or she can then click on the iPod under **Devices** in the left column and then click the **Summary** tab, as shown in Figure 3-6.

Viewing the firmware version of an iPhone does not require iTunes. An investigator can press the **Home** button, and then press **Settings**, followed by **General**, and finally **About**. The version number can then be seen, as shown in Figure 3-7.

Figure 3-7   The iPhone's version number can be seen on its **About** screen.

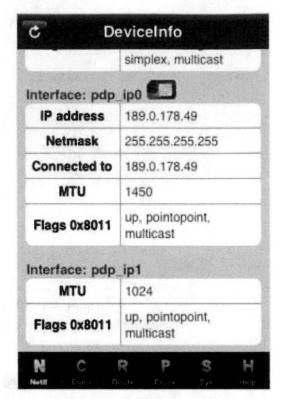

Figure 3-8   DeviceInfo shows network information from the iPhone.

Recover Network Information

Network information can be recovered using the DeviceInfo application for the iPhone, shown in Figure 3-8. It gives the following information:

- Network interfaces including VPN, GPRS/EDGE/3G, and Wi-Fi
- TCP/UDP connections
- Routing table
- Running processes
- System info, memory, and disk usage

Recovering Data from SIM Card

The iPhone's SIM card contains important information, including the following:

- Service-related information such as unique identifiers for the (U)SIM, the Integrated Circuit Card Identification (ICCID), and the International Mobile Subscriber Identity (IMSI)
- Phonebook and call information such as Abbreviated Dialing Numbers (ADN) and Last Numbers Dialed (LND)
- Messaging information including SMS, EMS, and multimedia messages
- Location information, including Location Area Information (LAI) for voice communications and Routing Area Information (RAI) for data communications

An investigator can recover SIM card data using the following tools:

- SIM Analyzer
- simcon
- SIM Card Data Recovery Software

Figure 3-9   The iPod has a calendar that uses standard vCalendar files.

Figure 3-10   The iPod can also store contacts using standard vCard files.

Acquire the User Account Information

The iPod keeps a record of the computer on which it is mounted. It stores the name of the computer and usernames of all users who have accessed the system while it was mounted. This information can be found with the iPod's name in several locations.

The DeviceInfo file, under a username in the iTunes folder, contains information about the computer with which it was used. This information can be used to verify the ownership of iPods.

View the Calendar and Contact Entries

iPods also possess limited PDA capabilities. They can be used to store calendar, schedule, and contact information. This information in iPods can be easily searched using a simple string search. iPods use the standard vCard file format to store contact information and the vCalendar format to store calendar and scheduling information. Calendar and scheduling information is stored in ICS files in the Calendars folder, while contact entries are stored in VCF files in the Contacts folder. These file formats store information in plain text format, which can be easily read.

Calendar and contact entries are stored with the file headers "BEGIN:VCALENDAR" and "BEGIN:VCARD" respectively. File headers indicate the beginning of each vCalendar or vCard entry and remain intact even after the file is deleted or the iPod is restored to factory settings. The iPod's Calendar is shown in Figure 3-9, and the Contacts menu is shown in Figure 3-10.

Recovering Photos

Because the iPhone uses iTunes to manage content, photos can be recovered using iTunesv8 by following these steps:

1. Connect the iPhone to the computer.
2. Run iTunes.
3. Click the **Photos** tab.
4. On the menu bar, click **Edit** and then **Preferences**. In the **Advanced** tab, you can specify the folder on which to sync photos on the computer.
5. Alternatively, use the Cellebrite UME-36Pro (a device used to transfer all forms of content, including pictures, videos, ringtones, SMS, and phonebook contacts data) to download the photos directly.

Recovering Address Book Entries

Address book entries can provide important information such as e-mail addresses and contact numbers. To recover address book entries, an investigator should follow these steps:

1. Check the address book entries on the iPhone in the following databases:

   Library_AddressBook_AddressBook.sqlitedb

   Library_AddressBook_AddressBookImages.sqlitedb

2. Retrieve the databases using iTunes on another computer.

3. Use tools such as Cellebrite UME-36Pro and WOLF to recover address book entries.

Recovering Calendar Events

Calendar events stored on the iPhone can provide information such as scheduling, meeting venues, and appointments. This sensitive information may be deleted by an attacker or the user. Investigators can recover the information by following these steps:

1. Check the Library_Calendar_Calendar.sqlitedb database on the iPhone.

2. Retrieve this database using iTunes.

3. Use tools such as Cellebrite UME-36Pro to recover calendar events.

Recovering Call Logs

Call logs in the iPhone store the date, time, and contact name (if stored) of all sent and received calls. They can be recovered by doing the following:

1. Check the Library_CallHistory_call_history.db database on the iPhone.

2. Use a tool such as WOLF to recover the call logs.

Recovering Map Tile Images

To recover map tile images, shown in Figure 3-11, an investigator should do the following:

1. Check the map tile images in the following locations on the iPhone:

    Library_Maps_Bookmarks.plist

    Library_Maps_History.plist

2. Use the tool Cellebrite UME-36Pro to recover the images.

Figure 3-11   Map tile images can give
clues as to a criminal's activities.

Recovering Cookies

A cookie is a piece of information stored by a Web browser, such as the iPhone's Safari. It helps the investigator reopen the Web pages that were accessed by the user or an attacker. Investigators can take the following steps to recover cookies:

1. Check the cookies database in Library_Cookies_Cookies.plist on the iPhone.
2. Download the cookies to a computer during an iTunes sync process.

Recovering Cached and Deleted E-Mail

To recover cached and deleted e-mails, an investigator should do the following:

1. Check the following databases on the iPhone:

   Library_Mail_Accounts.plist

   Library_Mail_AutoFetchEnabled

2. Download cached and deleted e-mails to a computer during an iTunes sync process.

Recovering Deleted Files

Files deleted on an iPod are not really erased; they are just marked as deleted. The .Trashes folder in the iPod shows all the deleted files. These deleted files can be easily recovered by using various forensic tools. When the .Trashes folder is full or the folder is emptied, deleted files are moved to the .Trashes\501 folder. These files cannot be seen normally and look like they have been completely erased, but these files can still be recovered using various file recovery tools.

Forensic Information from the Windows Registry

If the iPod is connected to a Windows computer, a great amount of information can be gained from the Windows registry. The registry maintains information about events occurring on the computer, including connection events with the iPod. The registry contains the following relevant information:

- Key created while connecting iPod to the Windows computer
- Last time when registry keys were changed
- Serial number of the iPod

The Windows computer creates a series of registry keys in HKEY_LOCAL_MACHINE\SYSTEM\CurrentControlSet\Enum\USBSTOR\ when the iPod is connected to it. Under USBSTOR, there are several keys, as shown in Figure 3-12. These keys determine the device's vendor, product name, and revision code. Directly under this key, there is another key that represents the iPod serial number, generally followed by "&0".

Forensic Information from the Windows Setupapi.log

The setupapi.log file is similar to the Windows registry in that it stores events such as driver and application installation. Setupapi.log records an event when the iPod is connected after system boot, but not if the iPod is already connected when the system boots. If the iPod software is not installed, the file records only the first time the iPod is connected, but if it is installed, then the file records every time the iPod is connected to the computer after system boot.

Generally, the registry key gives an accurate time of the last installation of the iPod drivers, as well as the time stamps of the setupapi.log file. If the iPod is removed and reconnected, the registry shows the time when the drivers were installed, while the setupapi.log file indicates the reconnection time. This information within the registry and the setupapi.log file can be used to create a partial timeline that will help in the investigation.

An excerpt from setupapi.log can be seen in Figure 3-13.

Recovering SMS Messages

To recover SMS messages, an investigator should take the following steps:

1. Check Library_SMS_sms.db on the iPhone.
2. Use the Tansee iPhone Transfer SMS tool for recovering SMS messages.

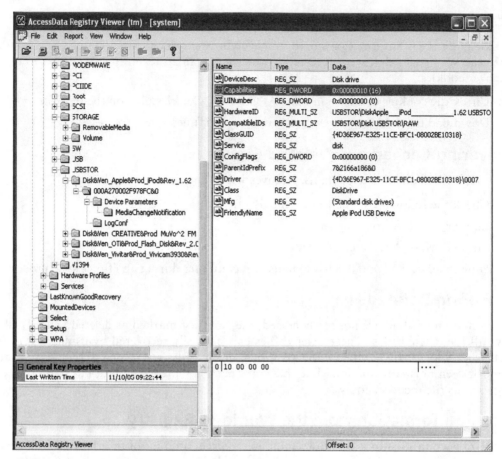

Figure 3-12   The iPod leaves several keys in the Windows registry.

```
[2005/11/10 20:07:44 3136.72]
#-198 Command line processed: "C:\Program
Files\iPod\bin\iPodService.exe"
#-166 Device install function: DIF_PROPERTYCHANGE.
#I292 Changing device properties of
"USBSTOR\DISK&VEN_APPLE&PROD_IPOD&REV_1.62\000A270002F978FC&0".
#I306 DICS_START: Device has been started.
[2005/11/10 20:07:50 3136.85]
#-198 Command line processed: "C:\Program
Files\iPod\bin\iPodService.exe"
#-166 Device install function: DIF_PROPERTYCHANGE.
#I292 Changing device properties of
"USBSTOR\DISK&VEN_APPLE&PROD_IPOD&REV_1.62\000A270002F978FC&0".
#I306 DICS_START: Device has been started.
```

Figure 3-13   Setupapi.log records additional information when the iPod is connected.

Other Files That Are Downloaded to the Computer During the iTunes Sync Process

During the iTunes sync process, the following other files are downloaded to the computer:

- Library_Keyboard_dynamic-text.dat
- Library_LockBackground.jpg
- Library_Notes_notes.db
- Library_Preferences_.GlobalPreferences.plist
- Library_Preferences_SBShutdownCookie
- Library_Preferences_SystemConfiguration_com.apple.AutoWake.plist
- Library_Preferences_SystemConfiguration_com.apple.network.identification.plist
- Library_Preferences_SystemConfiguration_com.apple.wifi.plist
- Library_Preferences_SystemConfiguration_preferences.plist
- Library_Preferences_com.apple.AppSupport.plist
- Library_Preferences_com.apple.BTServer.plist
- Library_Preferences_com.apple.Maps.plist
- Library_Preferences_com.apple.MobileSMS.plist
- Library_Preferences_com.apple.PeoplePicker.plist
- Library_Preferences_com.apple.Preferences.plist
- Library_Preferences_com.apple.WebFoundation.plist
- Library_Preferences_com.apple.calculator.plist
- Library_Preferences_com.apple.celestial.plist
- Library_Preferences_com.apple.commcenter.plist
- Library_Preferences_com.apple.mobilecal.alarmengine.plist
- Library_Preferences_com.apple.mobilecal.plist
- Library_Preferences_com.apple.mobileiPod.plist
- Library_Preferences_com.apple.mobilemail.plist
- Library_Preferences_com.apple.mobilenotes.plist
- Library_Preferences_com.apple.mobilephone.plist
- Library_Preferences_com.apple.mobilephone.speeddial.plist
- Library_Preferences_com.apple.mobilesafari.plist
- Library_Preferences_com.apple.mobileslideshow.plist
- Library_Preferences_com.apple.mobiletimer.plist
- Library_Preferences_com.apple.mobilevpn.plist
- Library_Preferences_com.apple.preferences.network.plist
- Library_Preferences_com.apple.preferences.sounds.plist
- Library_Preferences_com.apple.springboard.plist
- Library_Preferences_com.apple.stocks.plist
- Library_Preferences_com.apple.weather.plist
- Library_Preferences_com.apple.youtube.plist
- Library_Preferences_csidata
- Library_Safari_Bookmarks.plist
- Library_Safari_History.plist

Analyze the Information

The last step in an investigation is to analyze the data. Analysis includes the following:

- Find out the username and the computer the iPod is currently linked to for syncing operations by examining the \iPod_Control\iTunes\DeviceInfo file.
- Try to recover any hidden information.
- Use steganalysis tools such as Stegdetect to extract hidden information.
- If data is encrypted, use cryptanalysis tools such as Crank and Jipher to reveal the encrypted information.
- Use different audio and video players to view the audio and video files.
- Prepare a timeline of events of the iPod's connection to the system.
- If files are password protected, use Hydra and other password-cracking tools.
- Compare the timing in the registry or setupapi.log files with the event timings in the iPod.
- Open the data partition using a hex editor, and check the user's information such as contacts, calendar, and music files.

Timeline Generation

The investigator should create a timeline file during the investigation. Records of every activity are maintained in the form of time stamps in the iPod. The registry and setupapi.log files on the Windows computer connected to the iPod also keep records of every activity involving the iPod, starting from the first connection to the computer.

The timeline file should include the following information:

- \iPod_Control\Device\SysInfo modified time
- \iPod_Control\iTunes\iTunesControl creation time
- \iPod_Control\iTunes\DeviceInfo (and others) modified time
- When the iPod was connected to the computer and initialized
- Creation time for all music files
- Modification time of all music files

Figures 3-14 through 3-16 show how the time stamps on these files are generated.

Time Issues

Time is an important factor in the investigation process. The iPod has an internal clock, which will create a problem if it changes the file's creation and modification times. This clock should be tested using the following method:

- Set a different date and time on the iPod than that on the computer connected to it.
- Connect the iPod to the computer and copy some music files to the iPod using iTunes.
- Note the file creation, access, and modification times of the files.
- Disconnect the iPod from the computer.
- Check the time on the internal clock of the iPod.
- Play the songs on the iPod.
- Reconnect the iPod to the computer.
- Recheck the file creation, access, and modification times.

This can be checked again by copying the notes, calendar entries, and contacts to the iPod.

Jailbreaking

Jailbreaking is the process of unlocking the iPhone and iPod Touch to permit the installation of third-party applications. It opens up the file system of the iPhone so that it can be accessed from the computer.

Filename	Create Time	Access Time	Modify Time
\iPod_Control\Device\			
Preferences	Not set.	Not set.	Not changed.
SysInfo	Not set.	Set to midnight on day of connection.	Not changed.
\iPod_Control\iTunes\			
DeviceInfo	Set to time of initialization by iTunes.	Set to midnight on day of connection.	Set to time of initialization by iTunes..
ITunesControl	Set to time of initialization by iTunes.	Set to midnight on day of connection.	Set to time of initialization by iTunes..
ITunesEQPresets	Set to time of initialization by iTunes.	Set to midnight on day of connection.	Set to time of initialization by iTunes.
ITunesPrefs	Set to time of initialization by iTunes.	Set to midnight on day of connection.	Set to time of initialization by iTunes.

Figure 3-14   This chart shows how time stamps on iPod system files are determined while the iPod is connected and iTunes is running.

Filename	Create Time	Access Time	Modify Time
\iPod_Control\Device\			
Preferences	Not set.	Not set.	Not changed.
SysInfo	Not set.	Set to midnight on day of connection.	Not changed.
\iPod_Control\iTunes\			
DeviceInfo	Not changed.	Set to midnight on day of connection.	Set to time of closing iTunes.
iTunesControl	Not changed.	Set to midnight on day of connection.	Not changed.
iTunesDB	Set to time of closing iTunes.	Set to midnight on day of connection.	Set to time of closing iTunes.
iTunesEQPresets	Not changed.	Set to midnight on day of connection.	Not changed.
iTunesPrefs	Not changed.	Set to midnight on day of connection.	Set to time of closing iTunes.

Figure 3-15   This chart shows how time stamps on iPod system files are determined after closing iTunes for the first time in a session.

Filename	Create Time	Access Time	Modify Time
\iPod_Control\Device\			
Preferences	Not set.	Not set.	Not changed.
SysInfo	Not set.	Set to midnight on day of connection.	Not changed.
\iPod_Control\iTunes\			
DeviceInfo	Not changed.	Set to midnight on day of connection.	Set to time of closing iTunes.
iTunesControl	Not changed.	Set to midnight on day of connection.	Not changed.
iTunesDB	Set to time of closing iTunes.	Set to midnight on day of connection.	Set to time of closing iTunes.
iTunesEQPresets	Not changed.	Set to midnight on day of connection.	Not changed.
iTunesPlaylists	Set to time of copying music to iPod.	Set to midnight on day of connection.	Set to time of copying music to iPod.
iTunesPrefs	Not changed.	Set to midnight on day of connection.	Set to time of closing iTunes.
winPrefs	Set to time of connecting to computer for second time.	Set to midnight on day of connection.	Set to time of closing iTunes.

Figure 3-16   This chart shows how time stamps on iPod system files are determined after connecting the iPod to the computer for a second time in a session, copying music, and then closing iTunes.

Attackers use different techniques to jailbreak the iPod. After jailbreaking, they can install malicious code or software, which helps to access the information on the iPod. There are several tools used for jailbreaking, including the following:

- AppSnapp
- iFuntastic
- Pwnage

Tool: AppSnapp

AppSnapp jailbreaks the iPhone or iPod Touch and then pushes Installer.app to the device, which contains a catalog of native applications that can be installed directly over a Wi-Fi or EDGE connection. The jailbreaking can be accomplished purely using the iPhone, without interacting with a Mac or Windows computer. AppSnapp is pictured in Figure 3-17.

Figure 3-17 AppSnapp is a jailbreaking tool for the iPhone that includes the AppTapp Installer.

The following are some of the other features of AppSnapp:

- Patches SpringBoard to load third-party applications
- Activates non-AT&T iPhones automatically, while leaving already activated phones alone
- Fixes YouTube on non-AT&T iPhones automatically, while leaving already activated phones alone
- Installs Installer.app v3.0b5 on the iPhone/iPod Touch with Community Sources preinstalled
- Fixes Apple's TIFF bug, making the device more secure
- Enables the afc2 protocol and adds special commands to allow killing SpringBoard, Lockdownd, and others from the iPhone

Tool: iFuntastic

iFuntastic is an iPhone hacking and modification tool. It provides a GUI for almost any iPhone modification task. It can dig into an iPhone and edit images and logos, replace system sounds, and color iChat SMS balloons. It also has full file-browser feature, which simply browses the iPhone's internal file system.

iFuntastic can permanently jailbreak the iPhone. It has multiple home screen layouts, and it simplifies ringtone installation. The program is pictured in Figure 3-18.

Tool: Pwnage

The Pwnage tool is used to jailbreak both the iPhone and iPod Touch. It is shown in Figure 3-19.

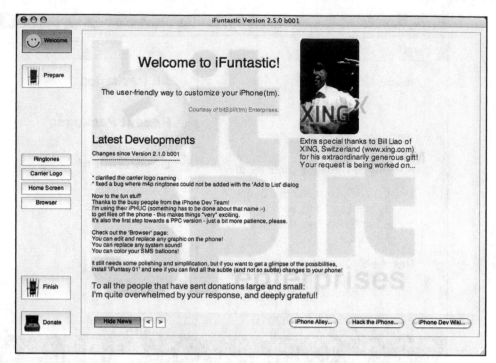

Figure 3-18   iFuntastic edits many aspects of the iPhone software.

Figure 3-19   Pwnage is a simple jailbreaking tool.

Tools for iPod and iPhone Forensics

The following sections describe tools used for iPod and iPhone forensics.

Tool: Erica Utilities for iPod Touch

Erica helps investigators extract different forensic information from the iPod Touch. The following are the tools included in Erica Utilities:

- *abquery*: Searches the address book by name
- *appLoad*: Forces SpringBoard to acknowledge new applications in the standard locations (/Applications and /var/mobile/Applications)

- *appSearch*: Searches the App Store from the command line using a simple query phrase
- *badge*: Badges application icons on SpringBoard with names, numbers, or anything else
- *deviceInfo*: Queries the iPod or iPhone for device attributes including platform name and processor
- *findme*: Returns the current physical location's latitude and longitude in XML
- *ip-print*: Shows the current IP address used by the iPhone
- *itmsSearch*: Launches an iTunes store search from the command line
- *launch*: Runs an application from the command line as if it had been launched in SpringBoard
- *notificationWatcher*: Listens for standard and/or Core Telephony
- *openURL*: Launches a URL from the command line
- *play*: Plays an audio file
- *plutil*: Property-list utility based on Apple's and expanded with extra functionality
- *recAudio*: Records audio from the onboard microphone
- *restart*: A nonlocking 2.0 safe version of restarting SpringBoard
- *sb*: A SpringBoard-specific utility that allows users to set, reset, and query SpringBoard preferences
- *sbar*: Tests status bar icons
- *tweet*: Sends an update to Twitter
- *urlclip*: Creates a Web clip (either normal or tel://) on SpringBoard from the command line

Tool: EnCase

EnCase recovers data from the HFS+ file system used by Mac computers and iPods formatted by Mac computers. It displays the file structure of HFS+ formatted devices, including hidden folders.

EnCase can be used on any OS with both Mac and Windows iPods. EnCase is able to extract deleted information from devices that have been restored to factory settings and have switched between HFS+ and FAT file systems.

EnCase automatically displays deleted files in an iPod. The Find File script can be used to recover deleted files, including images and Word documents. EnCase is shown in Figure 3-20.

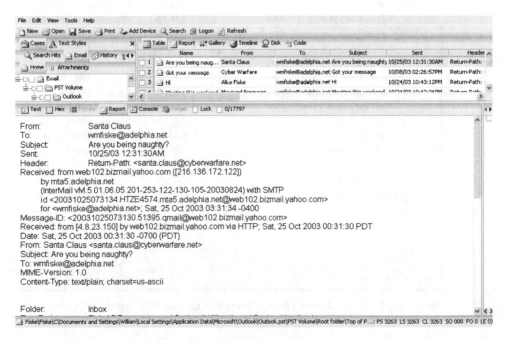

Figure 3-20 EnCase recovers deleted files from HFS+.

Tool: DiskInternals Music Recovery

DiskInternals Music Recovery recovers media files that have been deleted or corrupted. It supports most media types, data storage devices, and file systems. It can work even if the storage device was formatted and all information was erased, or if the information is corrupted.

Some of its features include the following:

- It supports a number of media formats, including MP3, WMA, ASF, WAV, OGG, WV, RA, RM, VQF, MID and VOC.
- It supports Windows, Mac OS, Linux, and other operating systems.
- It can recover files from hard drives, iPods, flash drives, MP3 players, CDs, and DVDs.
- It comes with an integrated media player so the user can preview files.

Along with the restored media, DiskInternals Music Recovery presents additional information. The utility provides a Music Slideshow feature that shows the tags and album covers of media files while DiskInternals Music Recovery scans for the deleted files. DiskInternals Music Recovery is pictured in Figure 3-21.

Tool: Recover My iPod

Recover My iPod recovers deleted or lost iPod files. Its features include the following:

- Recovers music, video, and images of M4A, MP3, QuickTime, and JPEG file types from any iPod
- Supports a range of iPods, such as iPod, iPod Shuffle, iPod Mini, iPod Nano, and other devices
- Recovers data from an iPod reset or restore

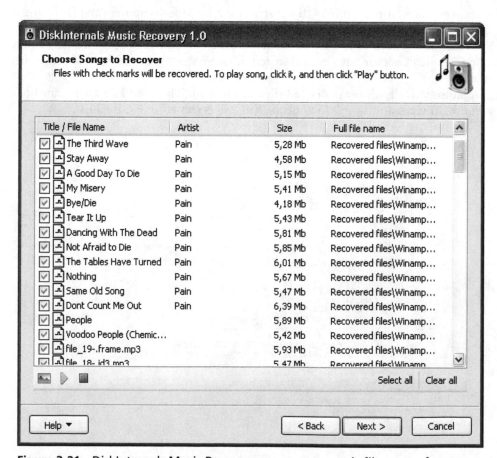

Figure 3-21   DiskInternals Music Recovery can recover music files, even from a formatted disk.

Recover My iPod has the following two search modes:

- A Fast Search of an iPod is used to quickly search for deleted iPod files.
- A Deep Search can recover all deleted, lost, corrupted, or unrecognized iPod drives.

The Recover My iPod search-results screen previews all iPod files that can be recovered, including full song title names, as shown in Figure 3-22.

Tool: Recovery iPod

Recovery iPod is designed to recover data from all iPods and is shown in Figure 3-23. Its features include the following:

- Recovers video files, audio files, image files, etc.
- Retrieves missing files from the Windows operating system
- Supports all Apple iPods
- Restores files that have been lost due to accidental formatting or deletion
- Retrieves files even if data reset operation is performed by the iPod
- Enables access even if disk partition volume is not recognized by the computer
- Recovers data if "drive not formatted" message is displayed on the computer while accessing the iPod as a disk drive
- Compatible with all versions of iTunes
- Supports iPods in all storage capacities

Tool: iPod Copy Manager

iPod Copy Manager can back up files from an iPod to a computer. It can also directly transfer files onto an iPod. The tool's user interface is shown in Figure 3-24.

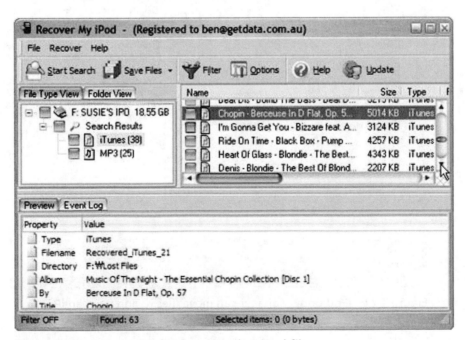

Figure 3-22   Recover My iPod recovers lost iPod files.

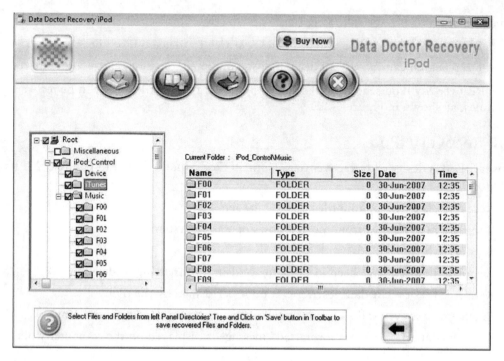

Figure 3-23   Recovery iPod can recover most data from any model iPod.

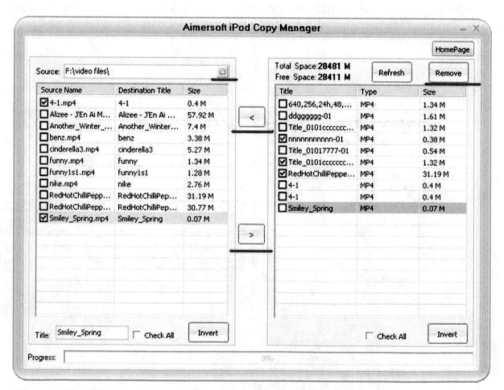

Figure 3-24   iPod Copy Manager can move files to and from an iPod.

Tool: Stellar Phoenix iPod Recovery

Stellar Phoenix iPod Recovery is another tool designed to recover all music files, graphics, videos, documents, and other files from an iPod. It is compatible with all generations of iPod and can restore the playlist in its original order after recovery. Stellar Phoenix iPod Recovery is especially useful in forensics because it runs in read-only mode to ensure the integrity of the evidence. Its graphical user interface is shown in Figure 3-25.

Tool: Aceso

Aceso downloads data stored in mobile phone SIM/USIM cards, handsets, and memory cards, and is pictured in Figure 3-26. Its features include the following:

- Handset access card creation
  - Blocks network access for all SIM and USIM cards
  - Prevents overwriting existing data
- SIM/USIM acquisition in single or dual mode
- Handset acquisition
  - 421 supported handsets, including Blackberry, Symbian, and iPhone
  - Data types supported: contacts, SMS, MMS, call registers, calendar, file system
- Memory card acquisition
  - Raw bit-for-bit image
  - File system

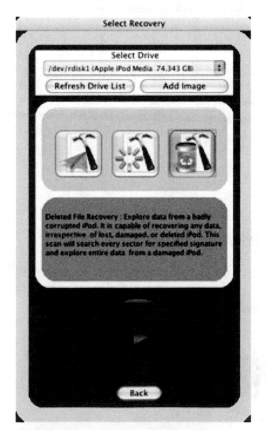

Figure 3-25 Stellar Phoenix iPod Recovery can recover files in read-only mode.

Figure 3-26 Aceso downloads data stored in SIM cards and memory cards directly from the phone.

Tool: Cellebrite UME-36Pro

Cellebrite UME-36Pro transfers the following types of data from mobile phones:

- Pictures
- Videos
- Ringtones
- SMS
- Phonebook contacts data

Its features include the following:

- Based on Windows CE
- Supports transfer of content across all mobile handset technologies, including GSM, CDMA, UMTS, 3G, TDMA, and IDEN
- Transfer of phone's internal memory and SIM card content
- Transfer of phonebooks, pictures, videos, ringtones, and SMS
- Supports multiple language encodings
- Available connectivity: USB, Serial, IrDA, and Bluetooth
- Transfer, backup, and restoration of mobile phone content
- Supports Symbian, Microsoft Mobile, Palm, and Blackberry operating systems
- Integrated SIM/smart card reader
- Integrated PC connection, allowing content backup and management
- Standalone device or an integrated PC solution
- User-friendly and self-explanatory
- Easily upgraded through software file downloads

Cellebrite UME-36Pro is shown in Figure 3-27.

Figure 3-27 Cellebrite UME-36Pro can transfer any kind of memory content from a mobile phone.

Tool: WOLF

WOLF can process iPhones protected by a security passcode without relying on hacking solutions that alter files on the device. Its interface is pictured in Figure 3-28 and can extract the following content without jailbreaking:

- Handset info
- Contacts
- Call logs
- Messages
- Internet information and history
- Photos
- Music
- Videos

Tool: Device Seizure

Device Seizure acquires and analyzes data from various mobile phones, PDAs, and GPS devices, including the iPhone. Text messages and images can be found in a physical data dump created by the program. Device Seizure, shown in Figure 3-29, can acquire the following data:

- SMS history (text messages)
- Deleted SMS (text messages)
- Phonebook
- Call history
  - Received calls
  - Dialed numbers
  - Missed calls
  - Call dates and durations

Figure 3-28   WOLF can extract data from an iPhone without jailbreaking.

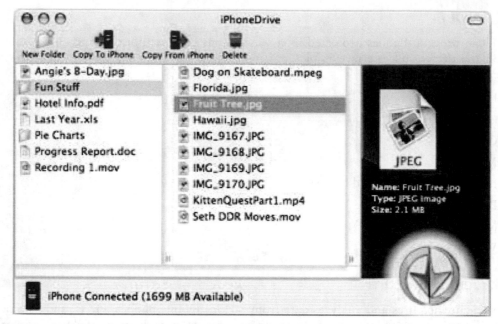

Figure 3-29 Device Seizure dumps the data from cell phones.

- Datebook
- Scheduler
- Calendar
- To-do list
- File system

Tool: PhoneView

PhoneView transfers files between a Mac and an iPhone, including iTunes media, photos, notes, SMS messages, call history, and contacts. It can add, view, and edit iPhone Notes on a Mac desktop.

Tool: iPhoneDrive

iPhoneDrive is a Mac OS X application that allows the use of an iPhone for file storage. Its drag-and-drop feature makes it easy to move files back and forth between the Mac and iPhone. iPhoneDrive's interface is shown in Figure 3-30.

Tool: Tansee iPhone Transfer SMS

Tansee iPhone Transfer SMS copies SMS text messages from an iPhone to a computer. It is pictured in Figure 3-31 and can export SMS messages in text file format or password-protected ANTS file format.

Tool: SIM Analyzer

SIM Analyzer, shown in Figure 3-32, is a lightweight tool for extracting the contents of a SIM card.

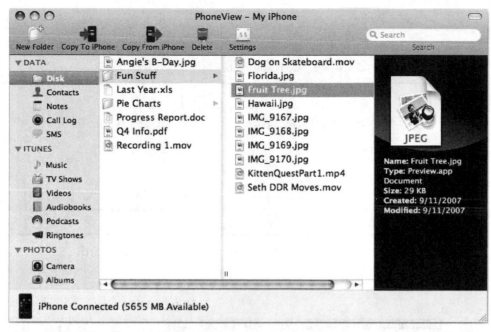

Figure 3-30   iPhoneDrive allows the iPhone to be used as an external storage device.

Figure 3-31   Tansee iPhone Transfer SMS exports SMS messages from the iPhone to the computer.

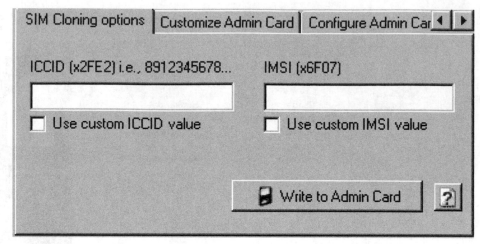

Figure 3-32   SIM Analyzer recovers the contents of a SIM card.

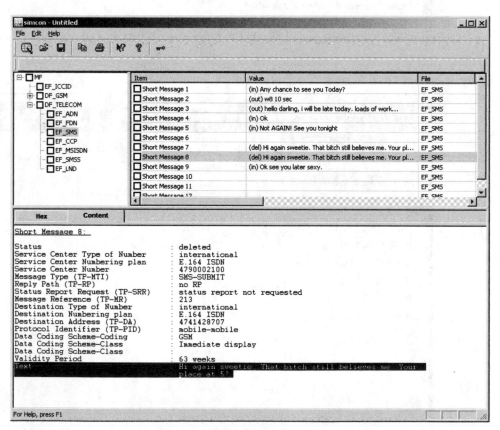

Figure 3-33   simcon makes an image of all files on a SIM card.

Tool: simcon

simcon securely images all files on a GSM/3G SIM card to a computer file using the simcon forensic SIM card reader. Its interface is shown in Figure 3-33, and it can perform the following functions:

- Read all available files on a SIM card and store them in an archive file
- Analyze and interpret content of files, including text messages and stored numbers

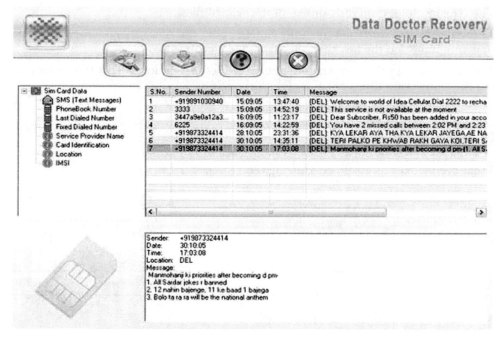

Figure 3-34   Recovery SIM Card can recover deleted SIM card data.

- Recover deleted text messages stored on the card but not readable on phones
- Manage PIN and PUK codes
- Use SIM and USIM cards
- Print a report that can be used as evidence based on user selection of items
- Secure file archives using MD5 and SHA1 hash values
- Export items to files that can be imported in popular spreadsheet programs

Tool: Recovery SIM Card

Recovery SIM Card, shown in Figure 3-34, recovers various types of deleted data from mobile phone SIM cards.

Chapter Summary

- An iPod can be used as a storage device as well as an audio and video player.
- The iPods formatted with Mac computers have Apple's HFS+ file system, and those formatted with Windows use the FAT32 file system.
- The iPod uses the standard vCard file format for storing contact information.
- Jailbreaking is the process of unlocking iPhone and iPod Touch devices to permit the installation of third-party applications.
- While unmounting the device, disconnecting or unplugging the computer might damage the device.
- Maintaining the integrity of the evidence is extremely important.
- Write blocking avoids alteration and maintains the integrity of data storage devices.
- The file \iPod_Control\iTunes\DeviceInfo in the iPod contains a lot of forensic information.
- The data partition on the iPod consists of all user information stored on the iPod.

■ The .Trashes folder in iPods shows all the deleted files.

■ The Windows registry contains information about the keys generated by the connection of the iPod to that computer and the last time these keys were changed.

■ The setupapi.log file is similar to the registry files in Windows. This file stores events that occur, including the connection time of the iPod to the system.

Review Questions

1. What are the basic steps in conducting iPod forensics?

2. What can a criminal do with an iPod?

3. What can a criminal do with an iPhone?

4. Describe the types of forensically relevant information stored on iPods and iPhones.

5. How can an investigator use the Windows registry in iPod and iPhone forensics?

6. What does the DeviceInfo file contain?

7. What does the SysInfo file contain?

8. What is jailbreaking?

Hands-On Projects

1. Use DiskInternals Music Recovery to recover media files that have been deleted or corrupted.

    ■ Navigate to Chapter 3 of the Student Resource Center.

    ■ Install and launch the DiskInternals Music Recovery program.

    ■ Explore the various options.

■ Click the **Next** button.

■ Click the **Finish** button.

2. Use Recover My iPod for recovering deleted or lost files from an iPod.

■ Navigate to Chapter 3 of the Student Resource Center.

■ Install and launch the Recover My iPod program.

■ Explore the various options.

■ Click the **Next** button.

■ Click the **Finish** button.

Chapter 4

BlackBerry Forensics

Objectives

After completing this chapter, you should be able to:

- Understand the basics of BlackBerry devices
- Understand the BlackBerry operating system
- Understand how the BlackBerry e-mail works
- Understand the BlackBerry Serial Protocol
- Understand the blackjacking attack
- Understand BlackBerry security
- Understand BlackBerry forensics
- Use BlackBerry forensic tools

Key Terms

Hash   a unique digital fingerprint of a document

Trackwheel   the BlackBerry navigation wheel

Introduction to BlackBerry Forensics

In 1999, Research In Motion (RIM) introduced the BlackBerry wireless handheld device. It provides a number of applications such as e-mail, text messaging, Internet faxing, and Web browsing, in addition to acting as a mobile telephone. The BlackBerry is a popular device, so it is often the subject of forensic investigations. This chapter will discuss how the device works, ways to increase its security, and what to do if it must be taken as evidence.

BlackBerry Features

The BlackBerry has a small, built-in QWERTY keyboard. It has a self-configurable AutoText feature that provides a list of frequently used words or special characters. The user interface is navigated using the *trackwheel*, the BlackBerry navigation wheel, along with a click function on the right side of the device. Certain BlackBerry models incorporate a two-way radio.

Modern BlackBerry devices have ARM7 or ARM9 processors, while older BlackBerry 950 and 957 devices contain Intel 80386 processors. The newer GSM BlackBerry models (8100 and 8700 series) have the Intel PXA901 312-MHz processor, 64 MB of flash memory, and 16 MB of SDRAM. CDMA BlackBerry smartphones are based on Qualcomm MSM6x00 chipsets and also include the ARM9-based processor and GSM 900/1800 roaming (as with the 8830 and 9500). The BlackBerry Storm's CPU board contains a new Qualcomm chipset with an MSM7600 528-Mhz processor.

These groups typically use the BlackBerry in the following ways:

- *Individuals*: Users can stay in contact with work and home.

- *Enterprise and government customers*: Professionals can keep in contact with their existing e-mail accounts and other enterprise systems.

- *Small and medium businesses*: The BlackBerry has the ability to address the wireless requirements of most businesses.

A BlackBerry device can be used in the following ways:

- As an address book, calendar, and to-do list
- To compose, send, and receive messages
- As a phone
- To access the Internet
- As a tethered modem, allowing notebook computers to access the Internet anywhere
- As an organizer
- For sending SMS messages
- For instant messaging
- For corporate data access
- As a paging service

BlackBerry Operating System

The BlackBerry's operating system runs on its microprocessor. It is event-driven, and supports multitasking and multithreading applications. If an event is triggered (such as a key being pressed or the trackwheel being clicked), the operating system sends a message to the appropriate application. When the application isn't performing other tasks, it checks for new messages using the RimGetMessage() function. When the operating system has no applications to process, the processor switches to standby mode.

Devices that connect to the BlackBerry require built-in RIM wireless modems. With the help of proprietary BlackBerry APIs, third-party developers can write custom software. However, these applications must be signed digitally in order to identify the developer.

BlackBerry software development was originally based on C++, but the latest models support MDS and Java. Java supports RIM devices that come with the J2ME MIDP platform. RIM provides a Java Development Kit that supports a custom application model different from the J2ME MIDP specification. The JDK consists of the javax.microedition and RIM's own net.rim.device.api package, which support a host of operating system–specific classes such as Bitmap, Application Registry, Keypad, Radio, and Persistent Object.

BlackBerry OS 4.7 is the newest version of BlackBerry and supports the following:

- Web standards including AJAX and CSS
- 1 GB onboard memory and 128 MB flash memory
- High-capacity, slim 1,500 mAh battery
- Tri-band UMTS: 2100/1900/850

- 3.6-Mbps HSDPA
- Wi-Fi technology (802.11a/b/g)
- GPS features
- Quad-band GSM/GPRS/EDGE
- Music synchronization
- Clock application

How the BlackBerry Receives E-Mail

The BlackBerry wireless e-mail solution works in the following four steps, shown in Figure 4-1:

1. The BlackBerry Enterprise Server (BES) constantly monitors BlackBerry users' mailboxes. When a new message arrives in a user's Exchange mailbox, BES picks up that message.

2. The message is compressed, encrypted, and sent over the Internet to the BlackBerry server.

3. The message is decrypted on the destination user's BlackBerry handheld. It is unreadable by any other devices, including other BlackBerry systems.

4. The server decrypts, decompresses, and places the e-mail into the Outbox. During this procedure, a copy of the message is placed in the Sent Items folder.

BES uses MAPI for communication with the user's Inbox. Using MAPI, BES immediately detects incoming messages. BES supports triple-DES security.

BlackBerry Serial Protocol

BlackBerry Serial Protocol backs up, restores, and synchronizes the data between BlackBerry devices and desktop systems. It is composed of simple packets and single-byte return codes.

The packets contain the following fields:

- Packet header (3 bytes, always D9 AE FB)
- Command type (1 byte)
  - 40 – normal command
  - 60 – extended packet
  - 41 – ACK
  - CF – handshake challenge
  - CE – handshake reply

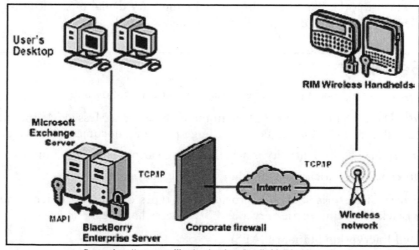

Source: http://www.mcgill.ca/ncs/products/handhelds/BlackBerry/how/. Accessed 2/2007.

Figure 4-1   The BlackBerry Enterprise Server sends e-mails from Exchange servers to wireless devices.

- Command (1 byte)
  - For normal command packets, a value of 00 specifies initialization-related commands
  - Extended packets always have a value of 02 for this byte
- Command-dependent packet data (variable size)
- Footer (3 bytes, always BF EA 9D)

Blackjacking Attack

Blackjacking is the act of hijacking a BlackBerry connection. Attackers make use of the BlackBerry environment to bypass traditional security. They attack the host of the network, usually with the BBProxy tool described below.

BlackBerry Attack Toolkit

The BlackBerry Attack Toolkit includes the BBProxy and BBScan tools, as well as the necessary Metasploit patches to exploit Web site vulnerabilities. The BBProxy tool allows the attacker to use a BlackBerry device as a proxy between the Internet and the internal network. The attacker either installs BBProxy on a user's BlackBerry or sends it in an e-mail attachment. Once activated, it establishes a covert channel between attackers and compromised hosts on improperly secured enterprise networks.

BBScan is a BlackBerry port scanner that looks for open ports on the device to attack.

BlackBerry Attachment Service Vulnerability

The BlackBerry Attachment Service in the BlackBerry Enterprise Server uses a GDI (Graphics Device Interface) component to convert images into a format viewable on BlackBerry devices. There is, however, a vulnerability in the GDI component of Windows while processing Windows Metafile (WMF) and Enhanced Metafile (EMF) images. This vulnerability could allow an attacker to run arbitrary code on a computer running the BlackBerry Attachment Service. Attackers can exploit this vulnerability with specially made image files.

TeamOn Import Object ActiveX Control Vulnerability

The BlackBerry Internet Service is designed to work with T-Mobile My E-mail to give BlackBerry device users secure and direct access to any combination of registered enterprise, proprietary, POP3, and IMAP e-mail accounts on their BlackBerry devices using a single user login account. A vulnerability exists in the TeamOn Import Object Microsoft ActiveX control used by BlackBerry Internet Service 2.0.

While using Internet Explorer to view the BlackBerry Internet Service or T-Mobile My E-mail Web sites, if the user attempts to install and run the TeamOn Import Object ActiveX control, an exploitable buffer overflow may occur.

Denial of Service in the BlackBerry Browser

A Web site creator with malicious intent may insert a long string value within the link to a Web page. If the user accesses the link using the BlackBerry Browser, a temporary denial of service may occur, and the BlackBerry device may become slow or stop responding altogether.

BlackBerry Security

BlackBerry uses a strong encryption scheme to safeguard the following:

- *Integrity*: Data integrity is generally maintained by using a Message Authentication Code (MAC) algorithm that produces a unique digital fingerprint of a document, known as a *hash*.
- *Confidentiality*: Confidentiality is achieved using various encryption mechanisms.
- *Authenticity*: Authenticity is assured by using digital signatures.

The BlackBerry Enterprise Solution provides two types of encryption techniques for all data transmitted between the BlackBerry Enterprise Server and BlackBerry handhelds:

- Advanced Encryption Standard (AES)
- Triple Data Encryption Standard (triple DES)

The BlackBerry encryption security mechanism meets U.S. military standards.

BlackBerry Wireless Security

The BlackBerry Enterprise Server keeps data encrypted during transit and ensures the data between the BES and the handheld is not decrypted anywhere outside of the corporate firewall.

The private encrypted keys are generated in a secure, two-way authenticated environment. These private keys are stored in the BlackBerry user's secure (Microsoft Exchange, IBM, Lotus, Domino, or Novell Groupwise) mailbox. The MDS (Mobile Data System) service acts as a secure gateway between the wireless networks, corporate networks, and Internet.

Figure 4-2 shows how this security works in corporate networks, while Figure 4-3 shows how it works with Internet servers.

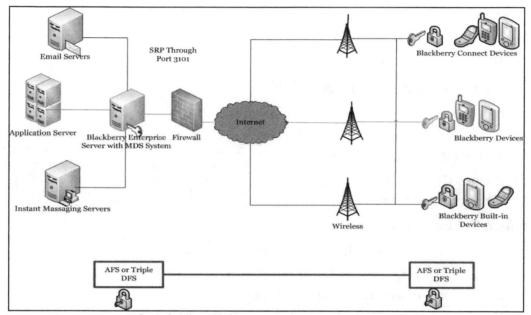

Source: http://www.BlackBerry.com/products/enterprisesolution/security/data.shtml. Accessed 2/2007.

Figure 4-2   This shows how BlackBerry wireless security works with corporate networks.

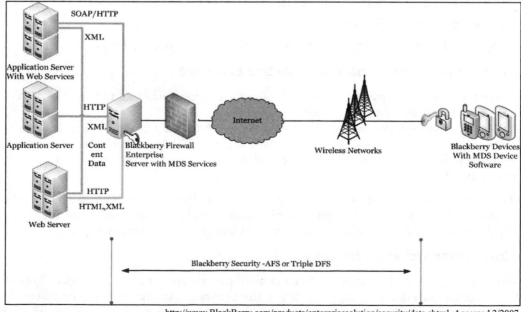

http://www.BlackBerry.com/products/enterprisesolution/security/data.shtml. Accessed 2/2007.

Figure 4-3   This shows how BlackBerry wireless security works with Internet servers.

BlackBerry Forensics

Prerequisites

The following hardware tools are recommended for BlackBerry forensic investigations:

- Faraday cage
- RIM BlackBerry Physical Plug-in
- StrongHold tent

In addition, the following software tools should be used:

- Program Loader
- Hex editor
- Simulator
- BlackBerry Signing Authority Tool

Steps for BlackBerry Forensics

1. Collect the evidence.
2. Document the scene and preserve the evidence.
3. Perform imaging and profiling.
4. Acquire the information.
5. Review the information.

Collect the Evidence

The investigator needs to seize the following items at the scene:

- Computer devices, including BlackBerry devices
- Memory devices such as SD and MMC cards
- Any nonelectronic evidence such as written passwords, handwritten notes, and computer printouts

While collecting the device, the investigator should take the following precautions:

- Use gloves, being careful not to disturb any possible fingerprint evidence on the device.
- Take care not to damage any evidence.
- Collect and keep evidence in bags.
- Do not allow unauthorized persons to visit the scene or touch the evidence.

Document the Scene and Preserve the Evidence

Document as much information as possible about the scene, including the state of all evidence. Take photographs of the scene and all the evidence present.

Evidence and documents must be kept in a secure, protected place in order to maintain the integrity of the evidence. Make sure all evidence is easily identifiable. If possible, label each piece of evidence with where, when, by whom, and how it was found. Secure the evidence from mechanical or electrical shock. Maintain the proper chain of custody at all times.

Radio Control Radio control can be used to control a device through radio signals. Therefore, the wireless functions of any devices must be turned off in order to maintain the integrity of the devices as evidence. This can be done either through the device's menu or by placing it in a Faraday cage.

Perform Imaging and Profiling

Imaging is the process of creating an exact copy of the contents of a digital device. This allows the copy to be analyzed rather than the original, protecting it from changes. An image should be taken of the file system using an SDK utility that dumps the contents of the flash RAM into a file easily examined with a hex editor. Program Loader, a piece of software used to perform most of the inspection in addition to taking the image, will cause a reset each time it is run. A reset can require the need for a file system cleanup, so obtaining a partition table risks changing the file system and corrupting the data. One way to work around this is to use the batch command. The batch command will group all command switches into a single access, avoiding multiple resets.

Acquire the Information

If the BlackBerry device is obtained with the power off, the investigator should leave it off until it can be examined. If the device is obtained with the power on, it is important to turn the wireless communications off, but not the device itself, for the following reasons:

- The BlackBerry is not completely off unless power is removed for an extended period of time or the unit is placed in data storage mode. Only the display, keyboard, and radio are shut down when using the GUI to turn off the unit.

- When the unit is turned on, queued items may be pushed to the unit before there is a chance to turn off the radio.

- A program might be installed on the unit that can accept remote commands via e-mail. This allows an attacker to delete or alter information.

If the device is password protected, that password should be obtained. However, the investigator should not attempt to simply guess the password; too many failed attempts may lead to a memory wipe. If the password cannot be obtained, the hardware should be read directly.

Hidden Data in BlackBerry Devices Data can be hidden on BlackBerry devices through hidden databases, partition gaps, and obfuscated data.

Certain databases that are custom written do not display their icon in the Ribbon GUI, enabling hidden data to be transported. The Rim Walker tool can identify such databases after being installed on the device itself. Once identified, the databases can be viewed by the savefs command in Program Loader, provided they are unencrypted.

The gap between the OS/Application and Files partitions can be used to store information. The partition table can be viewed using the alloc command in Program Loader, and space between partitions can be used with the savefs and loadfs commands.

Data stored at the end of the available file system space is retained after the device is reset and can be tested with the savefs command. This data can be viewed, but it cannot be modified.

Acquire Log Information The log-gathering procedure is in violation of standard forensic methods because it requires an image to be taken and then wiped from the record of logs on the handheld. Prior to applying the SDK tool, the investigator should access the logs present on the original device. Instead of the standard user interface, he or she should use hidden controls such as Mobitex2 Radio Status, Device Status, Battery Status, and Free Mem, to review logs.

- *Mobitex2 Radio Status*: Mobitex2 Radio Status (Figure 4-4) provides access to the following four logs:
  - Radio status: Shows the state of radio functions
  - Roam & radio: Records base/area (tower) and roam (channel) information with duration of up to 99 hours per base/area/channel; wraps at 16 entries and will not survive a reset; a blank entry represents a radio-off state

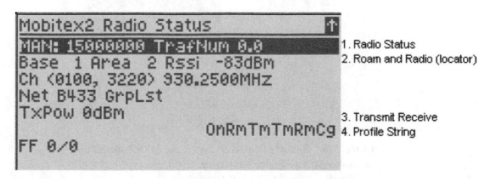

Figure 4-4   Mobitex2 Radio Status shows the status of radio logs.

- Transmit/receive: Records TxRx, gateway MAN addresses, type and size of the data transmitted, and both network and handheld date stamps per transmission
- Profile string: A recorded negotiation with the last utilized radio tower

To access the radio status, the investigator can use the following shortcuts:

- BlackBerry: Func+Cap+R
- Simulator: Ctrl+Shift+R

- *Device Status*: This function, shown in Figure 4-5, provides information on memory allocation, port status, file system allocation, and CPU WatchPuppy. The investigator can select a line in the Device Status using the trackwheel to see detailed information and to access logs. The investigator can access Device Status using the following shortcuts:

- BlackBerry: Func+Cap+B (or V)
- Simulator: Ctrl+Shift+B (or V)

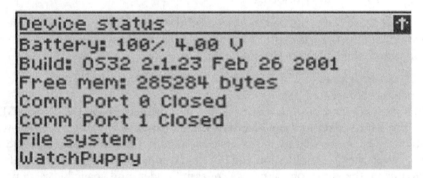

Figure 4-5   Device Status shows various information regarding the status of the BlackBerry hardware.

- *Battery Status*: Battery Status, shown in Figure 4-6, provides information on battery type, load, status, and even temperature.

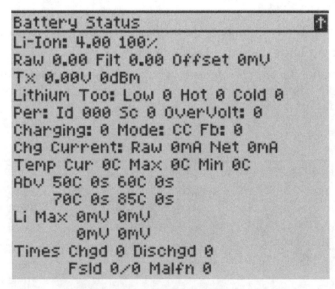

Figure 4-6   Battery Status shows various details about the state of the device's battery.

- *Free Mem*: Free Mem, shown in Figure 4-7, provides information on memory allocation.

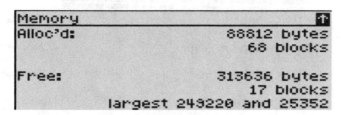

Figure 4-7   Free Mem shows information on memory allocation.

- *Comm Port*: Shown in Figure 4-8, Comm Port indicates the port's state. The security thread is not unique.

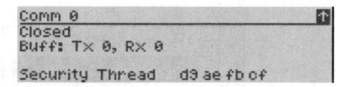

Figure 4-8   Comm Port shows the state of the port on the BlackBerry unit.

- *File System*: File System (Figure 4-9) indicates the basic values for free space and handles. The number of handles, which can be found in the SDK guides, is limited.

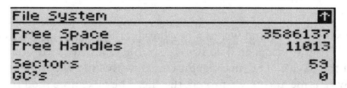

Figure 4-9   File System shows the basic values for free space and handles.

- *CPU WatchPuppy*: The CPU WatchPuppy, shown in Figure 4-10, logs an entry when an application uses the CPU past a predetermined threshold. It kills processes that do not release the CPU.

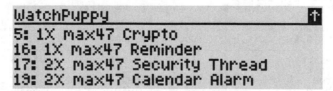

Figure 4-10   WatchPuppy logs programs that use the CPU past a predetermined threshold and kills programs that do not release the CPU.

- *Change To*: The Change To menu contains the over-the-air (OTA) calendar log. It is shown in Figure 4-11 and logs the last items synchronized via wireless calendaring on 32 lines, as well as providing access to debugging information.

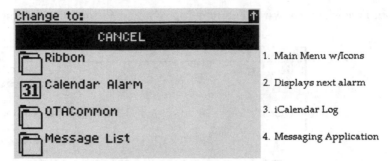

1. Main Menu w/Icons

2. Displays next alarm

3. iCalendar Log

4. Messaging Application

Figure 4-11 Change To contains the OTA calendar log.

- *Halt & Reset*: A reset causes the unit to reread the file system and can trigger a file system cleanup (Figure 4-12). The items marked as deleted during cleanup will be permanently deleted. This needs to be avoided for forensic investigation.

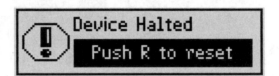

Figure 4-12 A reset will permanently delete any files marked as deleted, making them more difficult to recover.

Program Loader Program Loader is a command-line tool for imaging and analysis, containing the following commands:

- **savefs:** The savefs command writes a hex dump of the flash RAM to FILESYS.DMP in the same directory as Program Loader. The size of this file will be exactly equal to the amount of flash RAM available in the device. The investigator can view this file with any hex editor. He or she should immediately rename and write-protect the file. The next time the Program Loader is run with savefs, it will overwrite FILESYS.DMP without warning. This is also a good opportunity to create a hash of the file in order to prove integrity later in the investigation.

- **dir:** The dir command lists applications residing on the device by memory location, as shown in Figure 4-13. This will be useful later when attempting to emulate the original handheld on a PC. The investigator should take note of any nonstandard or missing applications.

```
Release -8
Bootrom: 1.0.13.0
Hardware: "RIM Inter@ctive Pager for Mobitex (Intel)"
        NAME         | FLASH  | BASE    | RAM   | BASE    | THUNK  | BASE    |
=====================+========+=========+=======+=========+========+=========+
PAGER950.EXE         |  30000| 3fc0000 |     0 | 580000  |      0 |       0 |
---------------------+--------+---------+-------+---------+--------+---------+
Address.dll          |   fe00 | 3fb0200 |  1c08 | 580000  |    55c | 3ff6004 |
AutoText.dll         |   4f00 | 3fab300 |   654 | 581c08  |    408 | 3ff6560 |
CryptoBlock.dll      |   a4e0 | 3fa0e20 |  162c | 58225c  |    194 | 3ff6968 |
Database.dll         |   90e0 | 3f97d40 |    d0 | 583888  |     8c | 3ff6afc |
English.dll          |   8c50 | 3f8f0f0 |   1f6 | 583958  |     28 | 3ff6b88 |
Localization.dll     |   1610 | 3f8dae0 |     8 | 583b4e  |      0 |       0 |
Message.dll          |  2a510 | 3f635d0 |  3848 | 583b56  |    8fc | 3ff6bb0 |
ribbon.dll           |  16a80 | 3f4cb50 |  1e5c | 58739e  |    544 | 3ff74ac |
SecureTransport.dll  |  19bb0 | 3f32fa0 |   d60 | 5891fa  |    5a8 | 3ff79f0 |
SerialDbAccess.dll   |   1890 | 3f31710 |   104 | 589f5a  |     d4 | 3ff7f98 |
Transport_MDP.dll    |   53c0 | 3f2c350 |  15a0 | 58a05e  |     fc | 3ff806c |
UI32.dll             |  1c810 | 3f0fb40 |   8ec | 58b5fe  |     cc | 3ff8168 |
Calculator.dll       |   3bf0 | 3f0bf50 |   4c0 | 58beea  |    190 | 3ff8234 |
Calendar.dll         |  29f00 | 3ee2050 |  263c | 58c3aa  |     8cc | 3ff83c4 |
MemoPad.dll          |   3280 | 3ededd0 |   118 | 58e9e6  |    300 | 3ff8c90 |
---------------------+--------+---------+-------+---------+--------+---------+
```

Source: http://www.rh-law.com/ediscovery/BlackBerry.pdf. Accessed 2/2007.

Figure 4-13 The dir command lists applications by memory location.

- **ver:** The ver command lists applications residing on the handheld and corresponding version numbers, as shown in Figure 4-14. This will be useful later when attempting to emulate the original handheld on a PC. The investigator should take note of any nonstandard or missing applications.

```
Hardware: "RIM Inter@ctive Pager for Mobitex (Intel)"

File Versions:

          NAME          |       VERSION        |    DATE    |    TIME    |
========================+======================+============+===========+
PAGER950.EXE            |  2,   1,  23,    0   |            |           |
------------------------+----------------------+------------+-----------+
Address.dll             |  2,   1,   2,   17   | 2001:08:23 | 17:26:22  |
AutoText.dll            |  2,   1,   2,   17   | 2001:08:23 | 17:26:03  |
CryptoBlock.dll         |  2,   1,   2,   17   | 2001:08:23 | 17:33:57  |
Database.dll            |  2,   1,   2,   17   | 2001:08:23 | 17:25:04  |
English.dll             |  2,   1,   2,   17   | 2001:08:23 | 17:36:16  |
Localization.dll        |  2,   1,   2,   17   | 2001:08:23 | 17:36:28  |
Message.dll             |  2,   1,   2,   17   | 2001:08:23 | 17:35:28  |
ribbon.dll              |  2,   1,   2,   17   | 2001:08:23 | 17:25:53  |
SecureTransport.dll     |  2,   1,   2,   17   | 2001:08:23 | 17:34:24  |
SerialDbAccess.dll      |  2,   1,   2,   17   | 2001:08:23 | 17:34:29  |
Transport_MDP.dll       |  2,   1,   2,   17   | 2001:08:23 | 17:33:46  |
UI32.dll                |  2,   1,   2,   17   | 2001:08:23 | 17:25:24  |
Calculator.dll          |  2,   1,   2,   17   | 2001:08:23 | 17:33:37  |
Calendar.dll            |  2,   1,   2,   17   | 2001:08:23 | 17:36:12  |
MemoPad.dll             |  2,   1,   2,   17   | 2001:08:23 | 17:36:36  |
------------------------+----------------------+------------+-----------+

API Versions:

Address.dll:
  Exports:   Address        2.1.2.17   -   Minimum Compatible: 2.0
  Imports:   Message        2.0
  Imports:   Options        2.0
  Imports:   UI32           2.0
  Imports:   Ribbon         2.0
  Imports:   Database       2.0
  Imports:   AutoText       2.0

AutoText.dll:
  Exports:   AutoText       2.1.2.17   -   Minimum Compatible: 2.0
  Imports:   Database       2.0
  Imports:   UI32           2.0
  Imports:   Options        2.0

CryptoBlock.dll:
  Exports:   CryptoBlock    2.1.2.17   -   Minimum Compatible: 2.0
  Imports:   Options        2.0
  Imports:   Database       2.0
```

Source: http://www.rh-law.com/ediscovery/BlackBerry.pdf. Accessed 2/2007.

Figure 4-14 The ver command lists applications with their version numbers.

- **map:** The map command displays detailed flash RAM and SRAM maps, as shown in Figure 4-15.

```
Release -8
Hardware: "RIM Inter@ctive Pager for Mobitex (Intel)"

FLASH MAP      (available flash = 1152 KB)

  from   |   to   |   size  |  name
=========+========+=========+=======================
 3fc0000 | 3fefff |   30000 | PAGER950.EXE
---------+--------+---------+-----------------------
 3fb0200 | 3fbffff |    fe00 | Address.dll
 3fab300 | 3fb01ff |    4f00 | AutoText.dll
 3fa0e20 | 3fab2ff |    a4e0 | CryptoBlock.dll
 3f97d40 | 3fa0e1f |    90e0 | Database.dll
 3f8f0f0 | 3f97d3f |    8c50 | English.dll
 3f8dae0 | 3f8f0ef |    1610 | Localization.dll
 3f635d0 | 3f8dadf |   2a510 | Message.dll
 3f4cb50 | 3f635cf |   16a80 | ribbon.dll
 3f32fa0 | 3f4cb4f |   19bb0 | SecureTransport.dll
 3f31710 | 3f32f9f |    1890 | SerialDbAccess.dll
 3f2c350 | 3f3170f |    53c0 | Transport_MDP.dll
 3f0fb40 | 3f2c34f |    1c810 | UI32.dll
 3f0bf50 | 3f0fb3f |    3bf0 | Calculator.dll
 3ee2050 | 3f0bf4f |   29f00 | Calendar.dll
 3ededd0 | 3ee204f |    3280 | MemoPad.dll
 3ed0000 | 3ededcf |    edd0 | [free]
---------+--------+---------+-----------------------

RAM MAP      (available RAM = 560 KB)

  from   |   to   |   size  |  name
=========+========+=========+=======================
  580000 | 581c07 |    1c08 | Address.dll
  581c08 | 58225b |     654 | AutoText.dll
  58225c | 583887 |    162c | CryptoBlock.dll
  583888 | 583957 |      d0 | Database.dll
  583958 | 583b4d |     1f6 | English.dll
  583b4e | 583b55 |       8 | Localization.dll
  583b56 | 58739d |    3848 | Message.dll
  58739e | 5891f9 |    1e5c | ribbon.dll
  5891fa | 589f59 |     d60 | SecureTransport.dll
  589f5a | 58a05d |     104 | SerialDbAccess.dll
  58a05e | 58b5fd |    15a0 | Transport_MDP.dll
  58b5fe | 58bee9 |     8ec | UI32.dll
  58beea | 58c3a9 |     4c0 | Calculator.dll
  58c3aa | 58e9e5 |    263c | Calendar.dll
  58e9e6 | 58eafd |     118 | MemoPad.dll
  58eafe | 5f6fff |   68502 | [free]
  5f7000 | 60bfff |   15000 | PAGER950.EXE
---------+--------+---------+-----------------------
```

Source: http://www.rh-law.com/ediscovery/BlackBerry.pdf. Accessed 2/2007.

Figure 4-15   The map command displays detailed maps of the device's memory.

- **alloc:** The alloc command displays a partition table listing the breakpoints between application memory and file system memory (Figure 4-16). The investigator should take note of any unused sectors and any difference between the end of the files area and the start of the OS and application area. If they are not the same, data could be hidden between the partitions.

```
RIM Wireless Device Command-Line Programmer Version 1.0.0.28
Copyright 2000 Research In Motion Limited
Connecting to device
Enter password (10 left):
Connected

Flash Allocation Log

Last valid entry: 0
  Files:        45 sectors at 0x3c00000
  Unused:        0 sectors at 0x3ed0000
  OS and Apps:  18 sectors at 0x3ed0000
  Fixed use:     1 sectors at 0x3ff0000
  1K Blocks:    18
  4K Blocks:     2
```

Source: http://www.rh-law.com/ediscovery/BlackBerry.pdf. Accessed 2/2007.

Figure 4-16   The alloc command displays a table of the device's memory partitions.

- **batch** [filename]: The batch command groups the previous commands into a single communication session. All of the commands are compatible within the same batch, with the exception of the savefs and loadfs options, which must be performed on their own. Because of this, the image should be made with savefs before any other operations. If a password is required, the Wpassword switch can be used, either on the command line or on the first line of the batch file.

Review the Information

Using a hex dump, there are two options to review the information:

- Manually review the hex files using a hex editor. This enables access to the entire file system, including the deleted records (indicated by byte 3 of the file header).

- Load the hex file into the BlackBerry SDK Simulator for review. The SDK can decode dates on any expired records.

Hex Editor Figure 4-17 shows a file dump created using Program Loader's savefs.

Simulator The BlackBerry SDK Simulator operates in exactly the same manner as a handheld BlackBerry; however, it is controlled on a PC with the convenience of a full keyboard. Dump files can be loaded into the simulator without handling the original unit. To use the simulator, follow these steps:

1. Rename the FILESYS.DMP file.

2. When the program loads, if the DMP file is in the same directory as the simulator and all simulator options are set to match, the file will be loaded instead of the default blank file system. The file will be overwritten to match the last state of the simulator while exiting the simulator, so ensure that it is not set to read-only.

3. Set the simulator to exactly match its flash memory size to that of the DMP file, as shown in Figure 4-18.

4. Set the simulator to match the network and model of the investigated unit, as shown in Figure 4-19.

5. Set the simulator to prompt for applications, as shown in Figure 4-20, and load the applications from those available in the SDK. The dir listing will help with this step.

```
Offset     0  1  2  3  4  5  6  7   8  9  A  B  C  D  E  F
00000000  2F 00 32 57 04 4F 04 FF  FF 0A 01 00 95 EB 27 08   .2W.O.ÿÿ...ë'.
00000010  0F 01 0D 00 FF FF FF 7F  FF 00 01 01 00 6B 63 63   ....ÿÿÿ ÿ....kcc
00000020  00 10 0B 05 00 54 65 73  74 00 11 0C 05 00 54 65   .....Test.....Te
00000030  73 74 00 FF FF FC FF 14  DB                        st.ÿÿüÿ.Û
```

Source: http://www.rh-law.com/ediscovery/BlackBerry.pdf. Accessed 2/2007.

Figure 4-17   This is a file dump created using savefs.

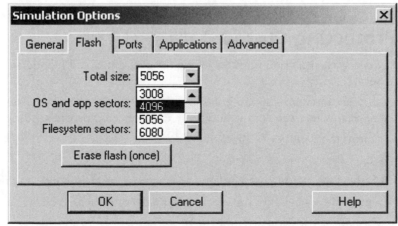

Source: http://www.rh-law.com/ediscovery/BlackBerry.pdf. Accessed 2/2007.

Figure 4-18   Set the simulator to have the exact same flash memory size as the DMP file.

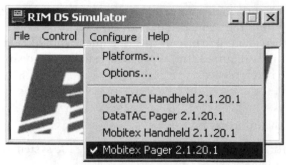

Figure 4-19 Set the simulator to match the
network and model of the unit.

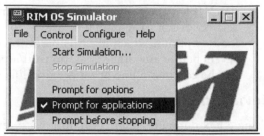

Figure 4-20 Set the simulator to prompt
for applications and load the same ones
used on the device.

Figure 4-21 This is the simulator running an
active simulation.

6. To run the simulator, click **Control** and then **Start Simulation**. The running simulator can be seen in Figure 4-21.

7. To connect the simulator to a serial port on a PC, run the following command: **OSLoader.exe OsPgrMb. dll /s1**

Checklist for Protecting Stored Data

- Make password authentication mandatory via the customizable IT policies of the BlackBerry Enterprise Server.
- To increase protection against unauthorized parties, there is no staging area between the server and the BlackBerry device, where the data is decrypted and collected before sending it to the BlackBerry.
- Periodically clean the memory of BlackBerry devices.
- Protect messages stored on the messaging server.
- Encrypt both the application password and the memory on the BlackBerry device.
- Protect storage of the user's data on a locked BlackBerry device.
- Limit password authentication attempts to 10.
- Use AES (Advanced Encryption Standard) technology to secure password entries, such as banking passwords and PINs, on the BlackBerry device.

Additional BlackBerry Forensic Tools

BlackBerry Signing Authority Tool

The BlackBerry Signing Authority Tool enables developers to protect the data and intellectual property of their applications. Developers can manage access to sensitive APIs and data using public and private signature keys. Administrators can select and access specific APIs and data stores.

The administrator can configure the tool to either restrict internal developers or allow external developers to request and receive signatures to access specific APIs and data stores. Signature requests can be tracked and accepted or rejected based on administrator control. The BlackBerry Signing Authority Tool supports all versions of the BlackBerry Java Development Environment (JDE) and applications created for Java-based BlackBerry devices.

RIM BlackBerry Physical Plug-in

The RIM BlackBerry Physical Plug-in allows the following data to be physically acquired from BlackBerry devices:

- Address book
- AutoText
- Calendar
- Categories
- File system
- Handheld agent
- Hotlist
- Memos
- Messages
- Phone calls
- Profiles
- QuickContacts
- Service book
- SMS
- Tasks

ABC Amber BlackBerry Converter

ABC Amber BlackBerry Converter converts: e-mails, contacts, SMS messages, PIN messages, AutoText entries, calendar events, phone hotlist entries, memos, phone call logs, tasks, and more from IPD (BlackBerry backup) files to other document formats (PDF, HTML, CHM, RTF, HLP, TXT, DOC, MDB, XLS, CSV, etc.). It is shown in Figure 4-22, and its features include:

- Generates contents with bookmarks (in RTF, DOC, PDF, and HTML) and hyperlinks in the output file
- Supports column sorting
- Displays selected messages (or contacts)
- Supports advanced PDF export options
- Supports multiple CHM and HLP export options
- Exports messages to TIFF and multipage DCX
- Converts messages to EML in bulk, which can then be dragged-and-dropped into Microsoft Outlook Express
- Includes Web Site Creator for BlackBerry and Advanced CHM Maker
- Extracts text of MMS messages
- Exports Browser URLs and Browser Bookmarks
- Supports Extended MAPI

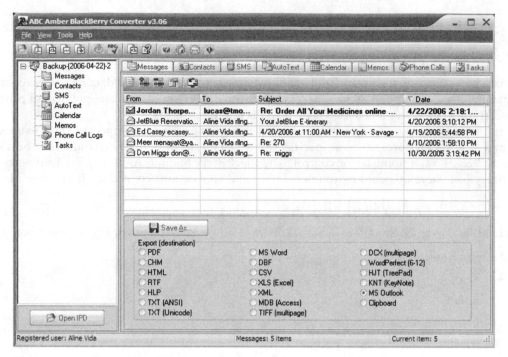

Figure 4-22   ABC Amber BlackBerry Converter converts IPD files into other document formats.

- Converts contacts to VCF (vCard), e-mails to MSG (Outlook), and calendar events to VCS (vCalendar)
- Allows a user to transfer e-mails to Novell Groupwise
- Includes command-line support
- Includes multiple language support

Data Doctor

Data Doctor is a Windows-based tool that can be used to collect data from all PDAs or equivalent digital devices for forensic analysis and scientific investigation. It can capture detailed information such as: Windows registry records, database records, mobile processor architecture, SMS messages, call history (call duration and call log), last-dialed and -received number, and saved files.

Data Doctor is shown in Figure 4-23 and supports all major brands of cell phones and PDAs.

ABC Amber vCard Converter

ABC Amber vCard Converter is a useful tool that converts contacts from VCF (vCard) files to many other document formats, such as PDF, DOC, HTML, RTF, and TXT. It is pictured in Figure 4-24, and its features include:

- Generates contents with bookmarks and hyperlinks in the output file
- Includes command-line support
- Supports column sorting in ascending and descending order
- Supports multiple PDF export options
- Supports multiple CHM and HLP export options
- Displays, saves, and prints selected contacts
- Includes multiple language support
- Exports contacts to TIFF and DCX (multipage)
- Converts contacts to IPD (BlackBerry)
- Converts contacts to Microsoft Outlook directly

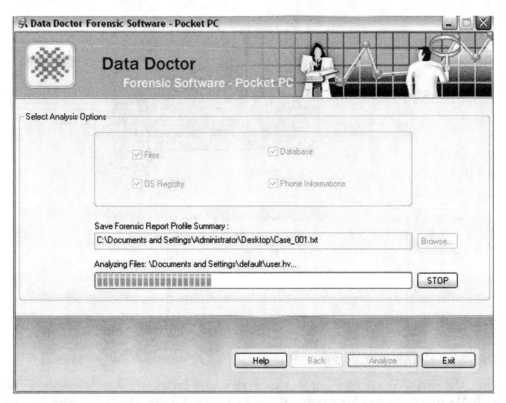

Figure 4-23   Data Doctor extracts all information from Windows-based mobile devices.

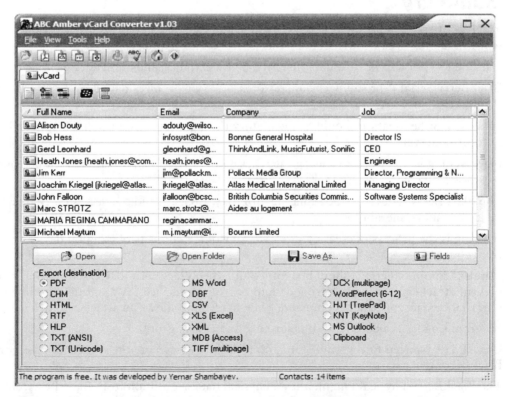

Figure 4-24   ABC Amber vCard Converter converts VCF files into other formats.

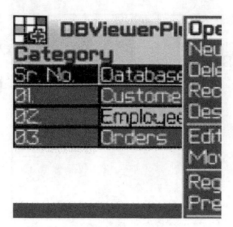

Figure 4-25   BlackBerry Database
Viewer Plus views and updates
database contents.

BlackBerry Database Viewer Plus

BlackBerry Database Viewer Plus can wirelessly view and update database contents on BlackBerry devices. It syncs with Microsoft Access, Microsoft Excel, and any ODBC-compliant database, including Oracle and SQL Server. The program secures data using 128-bit AES and is shown in Figure 4-25.

Chapter Summary

- The BlackBerry is a personal wireless handheld device that supports e-mail, mobile phone capabilities, text messaging, Web browsing, and other wireless information services.

- It uses encryption to protect data integrity, confidentiality, and authenticity.

- BlackBerry Serial Protocol backs up, restores, and synchronizes data between the BlackBerry device and the desktop software.

- Password authentication should be mandatory through the customizable IT policies of the BlackBerry Enterprise Server.

- Blackjacking is the process of using the BlackBerry environment to circumvent defenses and directly attack hosts on enterprise networks.

- The BlackBerry Attack Toolkit contains BBProxy, BBScan, and the necessary Metasploit patches to exploit Web site vulnerabilities.

- Imaging is the process of creating an exact copy of the contents of a digital device to protect the original from changes.

- Wireless communications should be turned off when BlackBerry devices are brought into evidence, to prevent attackers from transferring data to or from the devices. A program might be installed on the unit that can accept remote commands via e-mail. This allows an attacker to delete or alter information.

- Program Loader is a command-line imaging and analysis tool.

- Use AES (Advanced Encryption Standard) technology to secure the storage of password entries on BlackBerry devices.

- The BlackBerry Physical Plug-in allows physical data acquisition from BlackBerry devices.

Review Questions

1. How does the BlackBerry work?

   _____

   _____

2. What is BlackBerry Serial Protocol?

   _____

   _____

3. Explain the different types of BlackBerry attacks.

   _____

   _____

4. List some known BlackBerry vulnerabilities.

   _____

   _____

5. What are the steps for BlackBerry forensics?

   _____

   _____

6. How does an investigator acquire log information from BlackBerry devices?

   _____

   _____

7. What are some steps for BlackBerry wireless security?

   _____

   _____

8. What should be done to protect stored data?

   _____

   _____

9. Explain the various functions of the BlackBerry Enterprise Server (BES).

   _____

   _____

10. Describe the various components of the BlackBerry Solution Architecture.

   _____

   _____

Hands-On Projects

HANDS-ON PROJECTS

Remember to back up all data found on your BlackBerry device before performing these hands-on projects.

1. Visit the BlackBerry Web site.

   ■ In a Web browser, go to *http://www.BlackBerry.com*.

   ■ Explore the site.

2. Use Javaloader.exe commands.

   ■ Download and install a Java Development Environment (JDE) from *http://www.BlackBerry.com/developers/downloads/index.shtml*.

   ■ Run the program from a command prompt.

   ■ Give the following commands:

     • **javaloader -usb erase** to erase a module from the device
     • **javaloader -usb erase -f** to erase a module from the device, even if it is in use
     • **javaloader -usb wipe** to wipe the device (low-level format)
     • **javaloader -usb deviceinfo > device.txt** to save the device information to a text file (device.txt)
     • **javaloader -usb eventlog > event.txt** to save the eventlog to a text file (event.txt)

3. Use the BlackBerry SDK Simulator to emulate a BlackBerry device.

   ■ In a Web browser, go to *http://www.BlackBerry.com/developers/downloads/simulators/index.shtml*.

   ■ Download the BlackBerry SDK Simulator.

   ■ Install and launch the simulator application.

Index